"Possibly the best book I have read on an overview of the emerging church. It is so practical. I will be recommending this to everyone I can and will be using it as a workbook with our network leaders." – Jason Clark, Emergent-UK

"This is an excellent introduction to fresh expressions of church which engages with some of the key thinkers in the field. It is full of helpful examples, and, importantly, majors on the key underlying principles, rather than just offering models to be cloned. Highly recommended." – Graham Cray, Bishop of Maidstone and Chairman of the Mission-shaped Church working party

"Brimful of common sense, suggestions and spiritual nuggets. A must for any leader who wants to transition their people from passive church into exciting active church. A great book." – Christine Noble, *spiritconnect*

". . . challenging and practical." – Fran Beckett, Chief Executive, Church Urban Fund

"We need more and more concrete examples of how church can be done. Michael Moynagh examines the different approaches which people are making to address the culture in really effective ways." – Rev. Dr Rob Frost, Director, Share Jesus International

"A significant contribution to the critical debate about the future of mission-oriented church. Accessible and practical, it explores authentic Christianity." – Steve Chalke, MBE, founder Oasis Global & Faithworks

Revd Dr Michael Moynagh, author of the acclaimed *Changing World, Changing Church*, is co-director of the Tomorrow Project and a missioner with Fresh Expressions. He is based at Templeton College, Oxford.

The Faithworks Movement

Today sees opportunities like never before for the church to work in its rightful place at the heart of community. But it is not time for complacency. As the battle goes on for the place of faith in the public square, we must demonstrate that Christian faith does work and that churches are increasingly major providers of high quality social welfare that will benefit communities across the country.

Faithworks

Since its launch in 2001, Faithworks has sought to empower and inspire individual Christians, local churches and Christian projects to develop their role at the heart of their communities. To date thousands of individuals and hundreds of churches and projects have joined Faithworks in creating a movement that is both challenging the perception of the Church and delivering real grassroots change in communities.

Members can join as individuals, which is free of charge, or they can affiliate their church or Christian community project, for a small fee.

Faithworks Local Networks

Churches can achieve more by working together than they can alone – especially when seeking to liaise with and release resources from their local authority. A Faithworks local network is one way by which local churches can join together to create change in their community.

In essence, the Faithworks Movement exists to inpire and resource churches, Christian charities and agencies to live out their belief that faith works and to put faith back into the heart of the community.

www.faithworks.info

faithworks

emergingchurch.intro

- Fresh expressions of church
- Examples that work
- The big picture
- What you can do

MICHAEL MOYNAGH

With contributions by
George Lings, Stuart Murray Williams
and Howard Worsley

MONARCH
BOOKS
Oxford, UK & Grand Rapids, Michigan

First published in 2004 by Monarch Books,
(a publishing imprint of Lion Hudson plc),
Mayfield House, 256 Banbury Road, Oxford OX2 7DH
Tel: +44 (0)1865 302750 Fax: +44 (0)1865 302757
Email: monarch@lionhudson.com
www.lionhudson.com

Reprinted 2005

Published in conjunction with Faithworks

UK ISBN-10: 1-85424-664-X
UK ISBN-13: 978-1-85424-664-6
US ISBN-10: 0-8254-6068-9
US ISBN-13: 978-0-8254-6068-5

Distributed by:
UK: Marston Book Services Ltd, PO Box 269,
Abingdon, Oxon OX14 4YN;
USA: Kregel Publications, PO Box 2607
Grand Rapids, Michigan 49501.

Illustrations by Darren Harvey Regan

British Library Cataloguing Data
A catalogue record for this book is available
from the British Library.

Printed in Great Britain.

CONTENTS

ACKNOWLEDGEMENTS

I have written *emergingchurch.intro* mainly for people who are aware that fresh expressions of church are in the air and want to know more, for those who understand the concept but want to tease out the implications and for those who want to get started. Perhaps others who have been on the journey for longer will be encouraged by the stories of their fellow-travellers and stimulated by some of the questions raised.

I owe a huge debt to those who have been pioneering new forms of church, and who have shared their experiences in one way or another. The stories I have included are snapshots, taken at a particular time. It has not been possible for me to keep in touch with them all, but I have tried to draw attention to significant recent developments – especially if ventures have fallen on hard times – where I have been aware of them.

In particular, I am grateful to the following for their help, a number of whom also commented on the emerging text: Dave Barker, Canon Dr Christina Baxter, Jason Clark, Mark Griffiths, Revd Dr John Hall, Ven. Alistair Magowan, Revd David Muir, Revd Chris Stoddard, Bishop John Saxbee, Paul Thaxter and the CMS Mission Movement Team, Preb. John Wesson and Richard Worsley. In addition to their published contributions to the book, I have been greatly helped by Revd George Lings, Dr Stuart Murray Williams, Revd Bob and Mary

Hopkins and Revd Dr Howard Worsley. Shortcomings, of course, are mine.

St John's College, Nottingham, which has been a wonderful place to be, gave me a sabbatical, which created space to write the book.

As ever, my biggest debt is to my wife Liz, who has been a brilliant support and – despite her denials – has made the book possible.

Michael Moynagh, St John's College, Nottingham,
May 2004.

CHAPTER ONE

GOODBYE MODELS, HELLO MINDSET

Go to Halifax in the north of England, to a very ordinary Anglican church, at ll.30 on Monday morning. You might spot 30 or so people entering the building. They are arriving for a service of Holy Communion, after which they will have lunch together. The great majority don't attend church on Sunday. The assistant minister Kevin, who launched "Lunch Box", knew he was on to something when one of the men asked if he could be baptised during the Monday worship.

Nothing very dramatic there, you may think. But then many of the new forms of church emerging in the West are bite-sized and unobtrusive. Not very dramatic, however, does not equal unimportant. What helps to make these fresh expressions of church significant is that they are within reach of ordinary people.

For something entirely different, cross the Atlantic where soon you will never be late for church. In a 2003 *Christianity Today* article, Saddleback Community Church pastor, Rick Warren, said his church's future is in the Cineplex concept – multiple venues and worship styles, with a videotaped sermon, starting all through Sunday. Warren plans to double Saddleback's attendance to 30,000 per weekend, without adding any arena larger than its present 3,000-seat auditorium.

Near San Diego in Vista, California, the "video café" church has arrived. It started in 1998 with an overflow room for people who were last to arrive. Starbucks agreed to provide the coffee, and the room was arranged like a café. Soon the café became a worship service of choice. It was so packed that a second café was added, and then a third.

Now worshippers can choose from five worship styles at 13 services. In addition to "the main sanctuary", the outlying rooms contain edgy alternative, acoustical, lush praise and worship, and traditional. Each venue is more intimate than the main worship centre. "Leaders like it bigger, but the people like it smaller" comments pastor Larry Osborne.

When the live music ends, the video sermon is played. "We don't try to hide that it is on tape." After a few minutes, people don't notice that it is a video. Whether in the Chicago suburbs, in Atlanta, in Minneapolis, in San Diego or in Los Angeles, every experiment with this way of being church has found that people forget the preacher is not in the room with them. "The test", says Osborne, "is how do they respond when the preacher asks a question. Do they raise their hands when asked? Do they applaud a videotape? They do."[1]

This may not be everyone's café latte, but it is another, American-sized example of emerging church – new expressions of Christian community that have different shapes according to the culture in which they are planted. What is emerging church? Why is it shooting up the agenda? How is it different to other forms of church? Who is it for? And why do we need a book about it?

What is emerging church?

When I was a minister, I used to pop into our mums-and-tots group on Thursday mornings. I would watch the mums and carers scrambling after their babies. "How can I encourage them to come to church?" What I meant was "How can I encourage them to come to my church on Sunday morning?"

"We'll come to you"

Much of existing church operates in a "you come to us" mindset. Members decide what forms of worship they like. They fix a time that suits them. They meet in a building that they love (or is convenient). They agree their preferred shape for the service, throw in some of their favourite hymns and songs, and make sure the sermon is the right length.

Then, when the jigsaw is complete, they ask their friends, "Would you like to join us?" – an invitation to come to "our" church, set out as we like, at a time that fits us, on terms that we have pre-arranged. Sometimes churchgoers imagine their invitations are an expression of love. But if I threw a party for my child, would it be an act of love to put on what suited me?

"Emerging church" does not parachute a set model of church on to people: it is church from below. It starts not with a preconceived notion of church, but with the desire to express church in the culture of the group involved. It is church shaped by the context, not by "This is how we have always done it."

Some new expressions of church cater for Christians who are disillusioned with church. But a growing number are geared toward people with no church background. They start not with an invitation, "You come to us on our terms", but offer instead, "We'll come to you. If you want, we'll help you to be church at a time that suits you, in a place that is convenient to you and in your style, not ours."

emergingchurch.intro concentrates on this second category. It argues that emerging church could give Western Christianity a fresh and vital mission thrust. Its theme is how church can release this potential. But we must remember the bigger picture. Not all fresh expressions of churches are so mission-focused. Emerging church is a broad term, with many bedfellows. Key words perhaps are: contextual, customised, diverse, flexible and experimental.

Some examples

One former student from St John's Nottingham, England went as an assistant minister to a fairly traditional church. The Sunday services had almost no families. So he and his wife started "WOW!" – Worship on Wednesday.

> On a Wednesday afternoon children and their carers make their way from school to church. They have a drink, food and a quiz. Then they have a Bible story, followed by a bouncy castle, during which the mums and carers chat away. Finally, everyone goes into a church for a short act of worship.
>
> After about six months, some 40 children and adults were involved. Most were not attending church on Sunday. Some had already begun to think of WOW! as their church. The future? Plans were afoot to begin a Christian parenting class, as a step toward Christian discipleship for interested adults.

Another ex-St John's student described how the churches in his area had launched what was effectively a congregation for young teenagers.

> As the young teenagers got older, the congregation grew up with them, leaving a gap at the bottom. So the churches started a second congregation, for a new generation of young teenagers. The youth leaders were about to discuss what to do next. The older teenagers were becoming young adults. Most would not go away to college or university. So on the table was a proposal that the congregation for older teenagers evolve into one for young adults, the congregation for young teenagers mature into one for older teenagers and a third congregation be formed for a new generation of young teens.

A third student has just left college. She was asked to lead an *Alpha* course.

> In the final meeting, the group discussed church. "If church was like this, we'd come!" they said. So the recently ordained minister asked, "Why don't we make it like this?" They did, and they came – to "The

> Lantern". Between 20 and 30 meet on a Tuesday evening, sitting around tables and enjoying coffee and cake, some worship, "sound bite" teaching in a highly interactive style and the beginnings of other ingredients of church.

These are just three examples of tailor-made church – church that is shaped according to the culture and needs of the specific group. They are "mission" examples. Each caters mainly for people outside church.

Variety rules!

Emerging churches come in a dizzy array of shapes and sizes. New kids on the block range from GenX church, to children's church, to cell church, to pub church, to arts-based church, to post-Alpha church, to Menu-church and many more. Some are large scale and separate from existing church; others are small and integrated into the mainstream – a church-sponsored luncheon club, for example, that begins to include an element of worship.

Observer of the scene, George Lings, has described five bundles of emerging church (though any attempt to categorise is dangerous):[2]

- Some emerging churches plug into a network rather than a neighbourhood. Sid's Tattoo Parlor, on the borders of Santa Ana and Tustin, California, is a slightly intriguing example.[3]
- Another stream focuses on small groups as the context for church – base communities and cell church, for example.
- Other streams keep the congregation, but have changed where it gathers, when it meets and what takes place – such as alternative worship, some forms of café church, midweek church and youth congregations.
- Others engage in community development, where expressions of worship are low key and still evolving – a drop-in centre, for instance, which later spawned a small congregation.

- Some emerging churches mix-'n'-match these approaches.

Stuart Murray Williams writes:
Attempting to categorise the emerging church at this stage is like trying to nail jelly to a wall. The categories keep shifting as stories change, groups begin and evolve, and as our interpretation develops. But some attempt to describe and reflect is vital if we are to learn from what is happening.

Why "emerging church"?

Various phrases have been used to describe these expressions of church, such as "new forms of church", "new ways of being church", "fresh expressions of church" and "emerging church".[4] The lack of a single term reflects how cutting edge it all is – not even the language has been defined. Some emerging church pioneers would resist any label, lest they be shoehorned into a mould that doesn't fit.

Still inching ahead of the pack, perhaps, is the phrase "emerging church". Not everyone likes the term. Some think it is too passive, while others think that what they are doing is more than emerging church: it really is church. Stuart Murray Williams, well versed in the scene, prefers the label because:[5]

- it has the idea of emerging *from* somewhere – from existing church. This highlights the interdependence of "continuing" and fresh expressions of church;
- it strikes a provisional note – less a butterfly fluttering around than one still squeezing out of the chrysalis, which does justice to the state of play. Something new is happening, but what does it add up to? We need to keep learning;
- it is a dynamic term. New forms of church are emerg*ing*. This is a continuous process. Church is on a journey: it has certainly not arrived. So there is room for many more experiments. The fluidity of the phrase suits the fluidity of our emerging culture;
- it is an imprecise label. This resonates with many who are

experimenting with church and who feel that they have only just begun. They would recoil against a tight definition, which might box them into an expression of church they don't own.

For these reasons I have used "emerging church" in the title, thinking specifically of examples that reach non-churchgoers, but will interchange it with other labels in the rest of the book – flexi-language for a flexi-concept.[6]

Why is it on the agenda?

Attitudes are changing fast. A few years ago the concept of emerging church was very new. Now it is on many people's lips. As the existing church feels shaken and fragile, new expressions are crawling out of the rubble. It is too early to call this a renaissance, but the tectonic plates of church are on the move.

Spin the globe

In 2002, the Uniting Church in Queensland, Australia committed itself to God's transformation of church and to "understand that the viable future will be different from the church as we know it. Living this adventurous life of faith will mean fragility, tension and risk, but will also be characterised by openness and flexibility."[7]

In June 2003, at SoulFest Canada, a large Christian music festival, a one-day "Emerging Church Conversation" was held for those who were "actively seeking new possibilities to effectively engage and connect with their community . . ."[8]

"The Emerging Church Network seeks to begin a church planting movement among emerging cultures across the state of Texas." The Network is associated with "SemiNEXT Vision", which intends that by 2020 "there will be a global community of church planters and missional people learning from each other, as well as resourcing the specific needs of church planters and other missional people who lead the church in the first part of the twenty-first century."[9]

Rowan Williams, the Archbishop of Canterbury, has made new styles of church one of his priorities as Archbishop.[10] In early 2004, the Church of England's General Synod endorsed a report recommending that each diocese encourage and resource fresh expressions of church.[11]

The Google search engine identified over 616,000 references to emerging church.

The Great Revival let-down

Why is emerging church moving on to the front page? The simple answer is that the existing church is not making the grade. Today's church certainly has a future, but awareness is spreading that new forms of church are needed alongside it in a "mixed economy".

Church attendance in Scotland, for example, is expected to have plunged from 17.1% of the population in 1980 to 10.3% in 2005. The fall in Wales is projected to be even more precipitous, from 14.1% to 6.4% while in England attendance is predicted to nosedive from 10.1% to 6.7% of the population.[12] Church is not working.

In some circles hopes for revival intensified during the 1990s. But little happened. England, for example, had the "decade of evangelism" and the *Alpha* phenomenon. Yet the rate of church decline almost doubled![13] Some Christians became disillusioned. Others ask whether the Spirit is preparing the ground for more radical expressions of church.

The church disconnect

An Atlantic Ocean exists between the church and the surrounding culture. Church members struggle to cross it at work and in their social lives. They know their friends "will find church incomprehensible, irrelevant, archaic or twee".[14]

In its evangelism, the existing church tends to treat people as if they are the same. "Come to us on our terms, because we're sure you will like what we do" may have been appropriate in the standardised world of the 1950s and 1960s, when organisations treated people in a standardised way – the explosion of mass-produced goods and services was based on a one-size-for-all approach.

But it does not fit the new "customised" world in which diversity is celebrated. Test-drive a Smart car for example – look in the mirror and you think the back half has disappeared – and the sales pitch is likely to ignore how economical the car is and easy to drive. The emphasis will be on the huge choice of trims. The customer can have a model that is almost unique.

Marketers today take for granted that people are different. "Looking for a mobile plan that really suits you?" one advertisement asked. "Just pop into Vodafone and we'll help you find a perfect fit." In this it-must-fit-me world, Planet Church will be in outer orbit if it continues to treat everyone the same.

Jumping ship?

The church is also failing to connect with many of its own members. Excluding deaths and transfers, about 1,500 people are thought to be deserting the churches in Britain every week.[15] Many are long-standing members of the church. This is not the church shedding fat. This is eating away at the muscle tissue.

Alan Jamieson has conducted in-depth interviews with over 100 people who have left evangelical, Pentecostal and charismatic churches, mainly in New Zealand. He suggests that our postmodern culture's openness to doubt and questions, its ability to see truth as a complex paradox and its emphasis on relational networks, rather than impersonal institutions, is profoundly impacting many within the church.

A good number of people, often young adults, initially welcome certainty in a baffling world. Church provides a clear sense of meaning and well-defined boundaries. But after a while, culturally-in-touch Christians are forced to wrestle with the doubts, questions and perplexities of their contemporaries.

Black-and-white answers begin to jar. Previously accepted

beliefs and values start to be questioned. The certainty that was once appreciated in church becomes a straitjacket. Members are committed to church, but not – it feels – the other way round. The faith package chimes like a cracked bell.

The individual begins to clamour for an authentic church, with more room to explore the traditions of Christianity and more scope for the Spirit to shape their distinctive journey. A minority become "critics" of the existing church and want to move on.[16] They help to push alternative expressions of church up the agenda.

Although *emergingchurch.intro* is mainly about the potential of new forms of church to engage with non-churchgoers, we need to remember that these new forms can also help to prevent existing churchgoers from leaving. That, too, is part of the church's mission.

Or changing ship?

Some churchgoers have spent their whole lives on a waiting list for a better church. A large-church minister emailed me,

> Since we began the idea of launching a radical new congregation for Generation X, I have had quite a few not-so-young adults (40s and 50s . . .) asking if they can be involved because they also find church out of touch with their culture. I think that the Christians of our generation (the "Boomers") tried hard to fit into the culture of our parents, including the culture of church, while many of our contemporaries went off in a different cultural direction. We then brought up our children in a culturally-disjunctured church, and this became "normal" for us.
>
> As we take steps to set our children free to develop a style of Christian discipleship that will relate to their own GenerationX culture, guilt catches up with us. We realise (too late) that we should have done this ourselves, and want now to get on to the bandwagon. The truth is that there is still a job for us to do – to review our failure to address our own generation and to try to put that right, even at this late hour.

How is it different . . .

Haven't we been here before? What makes emerging church different?

. . . to New Churches?

Aren't new expressions of church, for example, just an updated version of house churches, now known in Britain as "New Churches"? Traditional churches were not connecting with the sixties' and seventies' culture, individuals felt stifled and so they broke away and started again. Weren't they pioneering "emerging church"?

The big difference, at least to emerging church in its mission mode, is that many New Churches continued to operate on a "you come to us" model. Members liked their new way of being church and used evangelism to encourage non-churchgoers to join them. They "souped up" the model of church but not the underlying approach: "We'll get a group of Christians together, express church in a way that we enjoy and invite others to come along."

Often they had considerable success. They attracted Christians from mainstream churches who might otherwise have dropped out. They appealed to lapsed Christians and people with some Christian background. Occasionally they drew in people with absolutely no experience of church. New Church attendance in England ballooned from 75,000 in 1980 to 248,000 in 2000.[17]

But New Churches have gradually drawn away from the secular world. Today, their sub-cultures can seem light years away from everyday life. Traditional churches may seem irrelevant to non-believers, but some New Churches can also look weird. Like their peers in mainstream churches, many young people feel out of place. As one leader asked, are New Churches about to become the quickest fossilised church movement in history?

Some New Churches have recognised the problem and have

begun to replace "you come to us" with a "we'll come to you" approach.

> Revelation on England's south coast, for example, has adopted more culturally current styles of doing church. "Our 'wineskins' have continually 'morphed'," the leaders claim, and now include "Warehouse", a youth and student congregation.[18]

Will Revelation and other such churches continue to "morph" in response to the fragmentation of modern culture? Or will they find new ways of keeping younger Christians in the fold, sigh with relief and ignore the bigger challenge of connecting with non-churchgoers?

. . . to church planting?

Emerging church is not quite the same as church planting either, although planting is at the heart of it.

In the early 1990s there were great hopes for church planting. Some thought that 20,000 new churches could be launched in the UK by the end of the century. In the event, between 1989 and 1998 only 1,867 churches opened in England, while 2,757 closed. Although a considerable number of plants were highly effective, a substantial number were not.[19]

Sometimes plants merely cloned the existing church. A group of Christians might move on to a housing estate or into a school, start perhaps a more relaxed version of mainstream church and then issue the invitation, "Come and join us". People came – some from other churches, some were lapsed Christians, one or two possibly had no Christian experience. But not enough newcomers arrived to sustain the new plant.

Numbers plateaued at 40 or 50, perhaps, including children. It became a struggle to crank up the pre-existing model of church every Sunday – to set up the hall, find musicians and give the children's teachers a break. Leaders burnt out. The plant either folded or stuttered along, exhausted. George Lings and Stuart Murray Williams comment, "The high failure rate of plants was surely related to replicating obsolescent models of church."[20]

Emerging church with a mission heart is different. It does not start with a pre-determined mould and expect non-churchgoers to compress in. It begins with the people church is seeking to reach, and asks "What might be an appropriate expression of church for them?" URC minister John Hall, who has researched youth congregations, comments, "The first Christian missionaries were Jews, and they struggled to *avoid* imposing their culture on their converts."[21]

. . . to cell church?

Cell church continues to mushroom. This is an expression of church based more heavily on small groups, each with perhaps eight to fifteen members.

Cells offer worship, learning on how to apply Scripture, pastoral care, ministry and evangelism, often organised around the four Ws: welcome, worship, word and witness. Cells may still come together for a weekly celebration, but cell becomes the epicentre of church life. Each cell is tasked with drawing in other people and multiplying. Some cells have a specific group in mind – the police for instance!

St Mark's Haydock, near Liverpool, is an exemplar of cell church in Britain. It had 300 people in 33 cells when cells were introduced in the late 1990s: five years later, cell membership had bounced to 500.[22]

Emerging church will certainly include cell church. But as proponents like Phil Potter are quick to say, cell church is not for everyone. E-church need not equal c-church.

Key to emerging church is that there is no one approach. Some forms of emerging church are based on cells. Others have a cell component – perhaps fortnightly cells that cluster together in the intervening weeks. Other emerging churches are not cell church at all. Diversity rules.

. . . to alt.worship?

Many people have equated emerging church with new forms of worship, not least "alternative worship". There is an overlap, but it is easily exaggerated.

Alternative worship started in Britain, then in Australia, New Zealand and the United States in that order, with some interest in Germany. "It is a small, fragile animal",[23] with groups of about 20 to 40, and extremely varied. Members long for more authentic community and worship than they experienced in mainstream churches.

Mission is not generally a high priority. Some groups are uncomfortable with blatant evangelism, seeing it as too directive and narrow. Others are so preoccupied with sustaining their new life that they have little time to reach out. The danger is that alt.worship groups will make little impact on their surrounding culture because they are so tied up with themselves. They could become another form of inherited church, updating the model but failing to take it on to the open road.

Does this differentiate "alt.worship" from emerging church? It would be misleading to over-define either. The reality is that not every emerging church throbs with mission, while behind alt.worship lie strong mission instincts, not least the desire to be contextual. Alternative worship has held people who might otherwise have abandoned church. Among those involved are individuals

> with an enduring sense of call to reach popular culture. In addition, they have a passion to close the divide between church and the rest of life. They seek to be responsive to post-modern culture, being in touch with preferences for ambiguity and antiquity. They also engage with post-modern instincts in the preferences for a multimedia approach which may be diffused not focussed, is created locally rather than remotely, works contextually rather than institutionally, makes use of the symbolic and the subversive rather than the didactic, and is open ended in style.[24]

Some in emerging church could learn from alt.worship's experiments in culturally attuned worship, while others in alternative worship might learn from "emerging churchers" who want to reach out. They share in common the desire to be authentic, to be contextual and to be community.

Although it will not be our focus, alternative worship is one expression of emerging church in its broadest sense – one series of experiments, along with many others, in what it means to sing God's song in a strange land.

> *George Lings writes:*
> *It is great that Mike shows the variety of examples of emerging church. But comparing emerging church to Cell or Alt. Worship is like asking how does a Citroen compare to a new car. The names are brands, the latter is a self-propelling mode of transport, in this case new. Emerging church is about releasing the kind of transport that suits where we want to go. The particular answer might be a Land Rover, a taxi or even a mountain bike. The whole point is to choose well for the mission you face.*

. . . to traditional church?

The essence of emerging church is a heartbeat rather than a formula. Emerging church does not declare, "We've done this. It's tried and tested. Take the model away and adapt it." It is more tentative, experimental and varied. Many involved are hesitant, unsure whether they have got it right and reluctant to make bold claims.

Not every seeker service, cell church, base community or whatever else is fashionable becomes a true expression of emerging church. Emerging church is genuine when it flees franchised, look-alike church in favour of more bespoke versions of Christian community. Some leaders spy something new and exclaim "That must be emerging church!" But emerging church is more than a new form of church: it is a culturally authentic expression of church.

Emerging church is a mindset ("we'll come to you") rather than a model. It is a direction rather than a destination. It rests on principles rather than a plan. It arises out of a culture rather than being imposed on a culture. It is a mood, scarcely yet a movement.

Stuart Murray Williams writes:

Hesitancy and humility are encouraging characteristics of many of those who are emerging churches, aware that they are exploring and experimenting. This is a refreshing change from those who advocate "this-is-the-answer" solutions, which have plagued churches in recent years. But tentative claims should not be interpreted to mean that they are playing at church – many are passionate, serious and courageous.

Sometimes people remark, "Traditional church serves people in their culture, so it's emerging church too!" *The Book of Common Prayer* can be an entirely authentic Christian expression of that particular congregation. But what prevents traditional church from becoming emerging church is the mission assumption – "come to us as we are".

When church members ask instead, "How can we remain true to ourselves but also sponsor a different expression of church alongside us, suitable for this group we don't reach?" then traditional church changes gear. It begins to move from inherited to emerging mode. Might the time come when Christians can say, "We are all emerging church now"?

Who is it for?

Is emerging church just for young people, or as one minister commented, "only for trendy, city-types"?

Not just the young

It is for all ages.

> For example, the Friendship Group for older people at St Alkmund's,
> Derby has grown steadily over ten years. It now has 70 to 80
> members. It meets every Tuesday in a church room for a two-course
> lunch, followed by a variety of activities one week and worship the
> next, on an alternating basis. A fortnightly Thursday group, with a
> dozen or so members, meets for Bible study. What makes this an
> example of emerging church is that the great majority of the
> Friendship Group do not attend Sunday church: what happens on
> Tuesday (and Thursday) is their church. The one-week annual holiday,
> involving around 30 members, is a highlight.

Not just suburbia

Café church, arts-based church, church in a David Lloyd leisure
centre . . . it could sound very middle class. But emerging church
is not for one part of society alone. Alongside experiments in
the suburbs, fresh expressions can be found in rural areas, in
city centres and among the urban poor.[25]

Often it is in places where the church is weakest that emerging church has most currency. In many areas of social disad-
vantage, for example, it is clear that the inherited church has
made little headway and so Christians are forced to try something new. Some of the most promising initiatives have been in
poorer urban areas.

Particularly among the urban poor, a growing minority of
Christians have experimented with different ways of being
church, using the insights of "liberation theology". They have
engaged with the needs of the poor, developed helpful method-
ologies for listening to their communities, adopted a process of
learning by doing and shifted from the congregation to smaller
groups, as the primary working unit of church.[26] Many have
experience in how to contextualise the gospel, and Christians
elsewhere might do well to listen to what they have learnt.

There have been heart-warming stories of individuals moving
on to housing estates, serving their neighbours and experiencing
a fresh expression of church as it spontaneously develops.

Two women moved into a housing estate in the north of England, and their home became a meeting place for neighbours. A small group now meets regularly, and those who come are finding out what "church" means for them. These are people who might be labelled "unchurched", and yet who are deeply interested in a way of being church "that is right" for that neighbourhood.[27]

A young couple described how they had been living in an unused vicarage on an ex-council estate. They had got to know a group of teenagers, invited them into the sitting room and found them all agog when they heard that the couple were Christians. "Does God answer back when you pray?" was just one of their questions. With the vicarage about to be sold, the couple had decided not to leave the estate but to buy a house there and open it to the young people. "We pray they will become a Christian community in their own style. Till we heard you speak, we didn't know it was called 'emerging church'."

Not just evangelicals

Pioneers of emerging church are mainly evangelicals. But there are a growing number of exceptions.[28] New forms of Christian community are not just for one wing of the church. Might fresh expressions of church blend the different traditions of mission?

It is only a slight caricature to say that evangelicals have traditionally emphasised the proclamation of the Word, with a view to encouraging individuals to make a personal commitment to Christ. Coming into a relationship with Jesus is vital.

Catholics have wanted to identify with people first, just as God has done through the incarnation, before inviting individuals to experience a community of love. The primacy of the church, as a corporate expression of God's love, is central to the pilgrimage into faith.

The liberal tradition has put a greater emphasis on promoting justice. You have to feed the hungry before you can evangelise them. Charity is all very well, but real change requires addressing the underlying causes of poverty, the ecological crisis and other social diseases. Social action is the priority.

Fortunately, these distinctions have been breaking down. All three traditions have much to teach each other. Holistic mission is becoming received wisdom. Yet much practice still belies this.

Many churches serve their local communities – perhaps through a drop-in centre, debt counselling or a place for young people to hang out. But for understandable reasons, they keep explicit Christianity in the wings. In contrast, some evangelicals continue to skip community development and go straight to evangelism. Too often, social action and gospel explanation remain on different sides of the road.

As we accelerate down the new century, church decline will make community development, shorn of evangelism, unsustainable. It will be like selling the family silver. Where will leaders and volunteers for community projects come from if the church continues to shrink? Liberals and others may have to make church growth a priority to sustain social engagement.

From the evangelical end, the widening chasm between church and culture will become ever harder to leap. As the numbers with no church background multiply (almost 96% of today's young people are not in church on Sunday[29]), more and more people will feel out of their depth in *Alpha* or the equivalent, if they come. Many won't have the slightest interest in attending in the first place.

Christians have close friends who practise New Age meditation or go swimming, but they don't join them just because they are friends. Likewise, people with no church background will not accept an invitation to an evangelistic event merely because it came from a friend. In our fragmenting culture, friendships in one part of life don't obviously spill over to the other parts.

So "friendship-based" evangelism will prove increasingly tough. The church may need to put in smaller steps to reach people outside church, serving them over the long term before sharing the gospel. And it may have to do this as an organisation if it wants to reach people as an organisation.

Non-churchgoers will be more ready to take note of church-based events that explain the gospel when they can say about church, "you are not like other organisations, you really cared". Friendship evangelism on its own will prove a weak model: church-based service, coupled with friendship, could be much stronger.

Stuart Murray Williams writes:

The term "friendship evangelism" expresses well the importance of relationships in sharing faith: most people come to faith in Christ through seeing faith lived out by someone they know and trust. But the term "friendship evangelism" is dangerous and might be better avoided: it smacks of manipulation, insincerity and ends-oriented relationships.

Almost certainly, these realities will force different traditions of church to try new ways of bringing social engagement and evangelism together. Christian groups are likely to experiment with novel ways of serving people. They will build expressions of community in the process. At the same time, they will look for acceptable ways of inviting participants to explore the Christian faith.

The result may be new forms of church that integrate social action, community and evangelism, as mission at its best has always done. Putative examples exist now. Might evangelical, Catholic and liberal approaches to mission enrich each other – and get a new lease of life – within an emerging church framework?

George Lings writes:

I'm delighted that Mike takes on board this acute need for actions before words, for the good reasons given here and developed in Chapter Seven. I'd want to add that in the cultures of spin and advertising, words are being devalued. People suspect they are used to gain power over them. Building trust through the integrity of loving service and quality community will be the key.

Not just those outside church

Emerging church, especially in mission mode, seeks to connect church to non-believers. But as we've noted, it can also cater for people inside church. Mark Oestreicher, who trains emerging church leaders in the United States, has written, ". . . I went through four phases in my thinking:

1. We've got to do something to fight this postmodern thinking in young people.
2. Wait a second; postmodernism isn't all bad, but it's still a generational thing.
3. Wait another second; there seem to be sixty-year-olds who are more postmodern in their thinking than some thirty-year-olds. Maybe it's not a generational thing.
4. Hey! This whole postmodern thing – it's me!"[30]

Not a few Christians go through a similar thought process. "I'm not too sure about emerging church . . . Well, it's not all bad and probably quite good for younger people . . . Hang on, it seems to be working for other people as well . . . Hey, it's for me!"

The big danger is that the existing church will turn in on itself. It will look for new expressions of church in response to the restlessness of current members. Keeping people is important – leeching members now is very serious. But it is not enough. It will not prevent further church decline, as we shall see.

So although some fresh expressions of church comprise mostly Christians, at its best emerging church will have non-members strongly in mind. Emerging church is the mission opportunity of a lifetime. Will it be a missed opportunity instead?

A new priority?

The theme of *emergingchurch.intro* is that fresh expressions of church should be at the heart of mission in the West. It assumes a strong theology of mission. In particular, it assumes that God is a missionary – that this is the very best reason for starting new forms of church.

Mission is at the heart of God

God engaged in a missionary act when he created the universe. Creation was an outward movement of God. It was an overflowing of the Trinity's life as something new was brought into existence. God continues in mission as he sustains the universe, a flow of non-stop love toward creation.

God also engages in mission by redeeming the world. This redemption is made possible through the death and resurrection of Christ. It continues through Christ, in the Spirit. God's purpose is to restore and perfect the whole of creation.

Mission, therefore, is no add-on for the church. The church becomes like God when it engages in mission. It falls away from God when it neglects mission.

Mission is at the heart of God's purpose for the church. The church is to participate in God's mission to the world. It is to be a mission agent of a missionary God. When the church ignores mission, it denies one of its main reason's for existence.

Western society has changed dramatically in recent years. In many places the church's mission is no longer to a Christian culture (if it was ever that), but to "post-Christendom".[31] This creates a missionary context that is cross-cultural – the church has to reach a very different culture to its own.

In this new context a balance has to be struck between the historic gospel, the particular culture of the church engaged in mission and the culture within which the Christian witness takes place. Sometimes the inherited church has been better at affirming the first two elements than the third.

The contention of *emergingchurch.intro* is that emerging church is vital to restore the balance. Indeed, the book goes further. It argues that church of a different timbre is key to Christianity's revival – perhaps survival – in the Western world.

A silver bullet?

But emerging church is not a magic solution. So often church leaders look for simple levers to pull: "Attend this conference or read that book, and you'll get the tools for reversing church decline." Life is seldom that easy. Church growth depends on many things – the work of the Spirit, prayer, pastoral care and competent leadership, to name some.

Emerging church is not a quick "pick-me-up" for a sick body. It is a collection of new vessels for all the ingredients that are essential to church – an "up" dimension in worship, an "in" dimension in community, an "out" dimension in mission and an "of" dimension, as individual churches see themselves as part of the whole body of Christ.[32]

Many of us have grown up with inherited ways of expressing these elements. At its best, emerging church is experimenting with fresh ways of holding these dimensions together.

What will the church look like in the years ahead? We need to experiment – to discover what it means to develop church bottom-up. We need to be urgent because the existing church is shrinking rapidly. We need to be optimistic because emerging church offers a promising alternative. And we need to be realistic – emerging church is no panacea.

A map of the book

I became interested in fresh expressions of church through my work on emerging social trends. It became obvious that society was leaving "traditional" church light years behind. Only if the church changed might it catch up. At the turn of the millennium I did some initial work on emerging church, but I kept wanting to know more.

emergingchurch.intro is far from a definitive statement: it is more a milestone on a continuing journey of discovery. What has surprised me is how many and varied emerging churches are, how complex are some of the issues they raise, and how much more I have yet to learn. I have written from a UK perspective because that is where I live, but from all I have read and heard Britain seems to be near the front of the Western world in church decline. As other countries travel in the same direction, maybe the UK's experience of emerging church will echo more widely.

Many churchgoers in the UK have jumped one hurdle – they have begun to embrace the idea of emerging church. But the next hurdle is coming up fast and is much harder: "Are we willing to pay for it?" Putting resources into new forms of church is about to become *the* strategic challenge.

The book's theme is that Christians should make fresh expressions of church a top priority.

- The values that might underpin emerging church, described in the next chapter, reflect God himself.
- Emerging church matters because of the changes in our society, some of which are explored in Chapter Three.
- It also makes good strategic sense, the thrust of Chapter Four.
- Far from selling out to consumerism, Chapter Five argues, emerging church has the potential to subvert it.
- Emerging church challenges us to rethink what we understand by "church" in today's world, the theme of Chapter Six.
- Emerging church is realistic – Chapter Seven suggests some practical steps individual churches can take.
- There is much that denominations and "streams" can do, the final chapter.

Emerging church is not the latest bright idea. It's a fresh way of thinking about church – and any church can do it!

Notes

1. "Let's go to the Tape", 17 June 2003, www.Christianity today.com/le/2003.
2. George Lings, "What is 'Emerging Church'?", www.emerg-ingchurch.info/reflection/georgelings.

3. Richard W. Flory & Donald E. Miller, *GenX Religion*, London: Routledge, 2000, Chapter One.

4. The pluses and minuses of these different terms are discussed in *Mission-shaped Church*, London: Church House Publishing, 2004, pp. 33–4.

5. In a conversation with the author.

6. Likewise I use inherited, existing, continuing and mainstream to refer to current churches: churches that already exist. "Mainstream" need not imply that emerging church must always remain a marginal activity. Fresh expressions can be a core task of church. Hopefully, many will become well established, and as such, part of the mainstream. These fresh expressions might then plant further expressions of church, the mainstream once again pioneering something new.

7. www.missionconsultants.ucaqld.com.au/postchristendom.

8. www.soulfest2003.ca/pages/sem/emerging.

9. www.emergingchurchnetwork.com.

10. See for example his speech to Church of England General Synod, 14 July 2003, available on www.emergingchurch.info.

11. *Mission-shaped Church*, op. cit.

12. Peter Brierley (ed.), *UK Christian Handbook. Religious Trends 4 2003/2004*, London: Christian Research, 2003, p. 2.24.

13. Peter Brierley, *The Tide is Running Out*, London: Christian Research, 2000, p. 27.

14. Stuart Murray Williams, www.emergingchurch.info/reflection/stuartmurray-williams.

15. Philip Richter and Leslie Francis, *Gone but not Forgotten*, London: DLT, 1998, p. xii.

16. Alan Jamieson, *A Churchless Faith. Faith journey beyond the churches*, London: SPCK, 2002, esp. Chapter Eight.

17. *UK Christian Handbook. Religious Trends 4 2003/2004*, op. cit., p. 2.24.

18. www.revelation.org.uk/info_history.

19. George Lings & Stuart Murray, *Church Planting: Past,*

Present and Future, Cambridge: Grove, 2003, p. 3.

20. *Ibid.*, p. 16.

21. John Hall (quoting Roger Bowen, *So I Send You*, London: SPCK, 1996, p. 76) in "The Rise of the Youth Congregation and its Missiological Significance", PhD thesis, University of Birmingham, 2003, p. 112.

22. "How cell was introduced to St Mark's Haydock", www.accn.org.uk/whatiscell/stmarkscell.

23. George Lings, "The Enigma of Alternative Worship", *Encounters on the Edge*, No. 12, Church Army, The Sheffield Centre, n.d., p. 3. For an introduction to, and resources for alt.worship, see Jonny Baker & Doug Gay, *Alternative Worship*, London: SPCK, 2003.

24. *Ibid.*, p. 21.

25. An example of emerging church among the urban poor would be Urban Expression (www.urbanexpression.org.uk), while St Thomas Crookes, Sheffield provides a city-wide example among largely middle-class folk. A number of rural examples are given later in the book.

26. See for example Jeanne Hinton (ed.), *A Tapestry of Stories: A New Way of Being Church*, Kew: New Way Publications, 1999. Other helpful *New Way Publications* are available from 25 Taylor Avenue, Kew, Surrey TW9 4EB. See also for example Chris Rowland and John Vincent (eds), *Liberation Theology UK*, Sheffield: Urban Theology Unit, 1995.

27. Jeanne Hinton, *Small and in Place: Practical Steps in Forming Small Christian Communities*, Kew: New Way Publications, 1998, p. 32.

28. One exception is "Contemplative Fire", an unfolding network of small cellular communities from an Open Catholic/Contemplative stable, within the Church of England's Oxford Diocese. Further details are available from philiproderick@btinternet.com.

29. See Chapter Three.

30. See Dan Kimbal, *The Emerging Church*, Grand Rapids: Zondervan, 2003, p. 58.

31. For an explanation of this term and reflections of the mission implications of being in "post-Christendom", see Stuart Murray, *Post-Christendom*, Carlisle: Paternoster, 2004.

32. Discussed more fully in Chapter Six.

CHAPTER TWO

SEVEN FACES OF GOD

Writing about "vintage Christianity for new generations", Dan Kimball remarks, "What comes into our minds when we think of the word church is the most important thing shaping how we function as church."[1]

Sometimes the lived-out values of the inherited church seem staid and stuck, and tell a dreary tale. Self-sufficiency is ingrained in the pews. Caution reigns rather than the thrill of trying something new. Status quo climbs into the pulpit. Comfort replaces sacrifice. Lack of imagination stunts the ability to reach out. "Make space for people who are different! You must be joking." Christian unity gets no more than a nod of the head. There are plenty of exceptions of course, but not enough to slay the despair of many churchgoers today.

This chapter lasers in on the very different values that can underpin fresh expressions of church. Describing these values is risky. Emerging church is a catch-all for a wide range of attempts to re-imagine Christian community. To imply that it is framed by one set of values could suggest a coherence that is not the case.

On the other hand, one attraction of emerging church is that it has the potential to reflect God himself. Accordingly, we start with the nature of God. Then we follow some of the high points in the story of God – creation, the incarnation, Good Friday and Easter, the Ascension and the great commission, Pentecost, and Christ's second coming. Emerging church is rooted in each turn of the story, which reveals a different aspect of God.

Interdependence

Emerging church risks dividing friends – being seen as a threat to traditional ways of doing things, or as a competitor for resources, or as the great hope for the future, leaving continuing church on the shelf. Sometimes emerging and inherited church are seen as different entities. Not true! They are interdependent.

Peering into God

Taking seriously the nature of God can help draw existing and new forms of church together. Recent theologians have stressed the mutuality of the three persons of the Trinity. The Father, Son and Holy Spirit are not just one in their love and respect for each other: as in all good relationships, their mutuality actually makes each other who they are.

In eternal relationship, the Father is the Father in the way he relates to the Son: he wouldn't be "the Father" if he had not chosen to relate to the second person of the Trinity as Father to Son. Likewise, the Son is only the Son because he relates as Son to the Father. The relationship between the first two persons and the third involves a sending out: the Spirit is sent by the Father and the Son.

This way of thinking about the Godhead affirms the distinctiveness of each person, but also puts an accent on their interdependence. For the church it provides more than a helpful model: God the Trinity invites believers to share the life of God's self. As the church does this, it values interdependence and difference.

An interdependent church?

Interdependence and difference should be the hallmarks of emerging church. "New forms of congregation may be planted, whether as youth mission or any other, but a relationship of interdependence is maintained with the original church. Each gives identity to the other. The youth congregation could not exist without the resourcing of its 'parent', but the founding congregation is no longer the same . . . a new dimension has entered its life."[2]

Just as the Father has handed the Kingdom to the Son, the inherited church may hand to emerging church the task of serving groups beyond its reach. Likewise, just as the Son will hand his completed work back to the Father,[3] so emerging church offers its accomplishments back to the mainstream.

This interdependence between the "generations" of church can take many forms. At the extreme, some traditional churches have become seriously senile. Younger adults may need to take control of the household. Less dramatically, newly formed churches may be able to give practical support to the wider church.

A church near Hull, for example, started an *Alpha* course. It was highly successful. The group continued to meet, as an expression of church. But for two years it seemed to spin off on its own. Then the group decided to contribute to the finances of its parent – the birth of hyphenated church.

Base camp people need frontiers people. Emerging church pioneers can afford to explore because others are stoking the home fires, while members of existing church may be more comfortable in their roles knowing that others are sparking new developments.

So there is no need for emerging church to be like a meteor squashing dinosaurs: on the contrary, it can bring new life into the church.

> Northern Community Church in Melbourne, Australia has
> mushroomed into several café congregations. One was primarily
> discussion based.

The members and leaders discerned the need for reflective and
contemplative spirituality, but attempts to incorporate this into
congregational worship met with mixed results. The congregation brainstormed about practices that were essential for individual spiritual development. It then vowed to regularly revisit
these spiritual disciplines and hold one another accountable to
engage regularly in them. The programme had a great impact
on the congregation as a whole and its individual members. A
year later the spiritual disciplines were adopted by the church
across all congregations.[4]

An emerging congregation invigorated the others, not least
the original parent.

Experimentation

> A rural church in the east of England had a thriving luncheon club for
> older people. Forty or so people attended regularly, hardly any of
> whom went to church on Sunday. One day a visitor popped in. He
> was so impressed, he suggested that after lunch was over they put a
> little table at the very front of the church, light a candle, play or sing
> some Taizé music, have one or two simple prayers, perhaps read a
> story from the Bible and invite those who wanted to gather round.
> The leaders pondered. "No harm in having a go," they said. To their
> amazement, nearly every person in that luncheon club stayed behind
> – the start of a new congregation? Their experiment had worked.

Part of life

Experiments are one of the defining features of emerging
church. Often people don't know what will take root in their
situation – or if church can be planted at all. They try something (sometimes anything!), and then learn from the results.

When this happens, pioneers take a leaf out of God's book.
For God has chosen experiments to propel creation. What is

evolution if it is not a history of experimentation? One species flourishes, another doesn't, a third mutates. It is as if each is asking, "What will work in this context?" The natural world is a living laboratory, constantly learning.

The same is true of human history. Civilisation is the product of successful experiments – houses that stay up, cars that work, banks that don't *quite* drive you to distraction and systems of government that are less awful than the alternatives. Some experiments have survived because there is nothing better; most of the flops have long been forgotten.

Experimentation is part of being human. So it should be second nature for Christians to "try and try again" with church.

The Great Experimenter

Some theologians would go further. They would say that the experimentation we see in creation reflects an aspect of God himself. God is an experimenter.

Does Genesis 2 contain a picture of God in experimental mode? He places Adam in the garden and then decides that "it is not good for the man to be alone. I will make a helper suitable for him" (vs. 18). He forms all the animals and brings them to Adam to see what he would call them. "But for Adam no suitable helper was found" (vs. 20).

Has God's experiment not succeeded? None of the animals provide a suitable partner for the man. So God "tries" again. He creates the woman, and this time the man lets out an exclamation of delight: "Now this, at last . . ." (vs. 23, NEB). The experiment has produced the desired result. God seems to be "learning".

Enrolling God as a learner makes some Christians wince. Doesn't it imply that he is not all knowing, one of the traditional characteristics of God? Some theologians have replied that God voluntarily limits his knowledge. God knows everything about the past and the present, and he *could* know everything about the future, but when he relates to creation he chooses not to.

Perhaps it is a bit like a parent reading their child a story. "Tell me what happens!" the child pleads. Of course the parent could turn to the last page, but they decide not to. They have the joy of sharing the child's roller-coaster emotions as the story unfolds.

It is part of God's perfection that he can be surprised by creation. He has created the notes, for example, but not the songs that humans compose. Each new chart-buster can amaze, and perhaps delight him. There is something uniquely thrilling about a wonderful surprise. Is God to be denied that emotion?[5]

George Lings writes:

I'm glad Mike has been this daring and picked up the open and creative relationship God has with his creatures, to which the Bible testifies and which makes so much better sense of a world where clearly things go wrong. I'd only add that God's grand experiment, or risk, was to choose to create beings who have genuine freedom to love him or not. All the rest flows from this audacious step.

Follow that!

God is presented to us as an experimenter, even a learner. So when emerging church experiments, Christians are not only being true to themselves, as creatures made to experiment: they are reflecting God's character. And when the rest of the church learns from these experiments, God's character is again on display. Fresh expressions of church provide an opportunity for the church as a whole to become more like God.

Sometimes the inherited church feels so pedestrian. But there is no need to stay with the church as it is. If it's not working, we can try something different. One youth worker leapt with joy when he discovered that God was an experimenter. His experiments with church gained a new legitimacy. The church can escape its envelope of caution.

Transformation

The big mountain for the church is to breed radical disciples – Christians who are willing to serve brittle and broken people rather than themselves, and who seek to be transformed so that they can transform society. Fresh expressions of church are not an ecclesiastical theme park, with fun on every ride. Many are in the business of change.

Culture-shaped

The youth workers vividly described their work with young people on a tough housing estate in the north east of England. It had taken them well over a year slowly to form relationships with the teenagers, but now the youngsters were beginning to come into their front room. Most of the young people knew absolutely nothing about Christianity, but were starting to ask questions and show interest. The youth workers hoped that gradually a congregation, in effect, would form in their sitting room and that eventually the young people would be discipled into radical expressions of Christian faith. "What are your priorities?" someone asked. "To keep them out of mainstream church" was the quick reply. Everyone understood what was meant. If the teenagers were to make the journey, church needed to be in their culture.

When the Son of God reached out to the world, he did not stand on the touchline of human culture. Through the incarnation, he immersed himself in first-century Israel. The culture of the day moulded the life he led – everything from the language he spoke, to the clothes he wore, to the places he visited, to his nationality.

The mission context shaped the form the incarnation took, and a similar process is true of emerging churches today. They allow their expressions of church to be shaped by the cultures they are in.

The God for all cultures dived into one particular culture. By becoming human, the Son could be in only one place at one time. The church is commissioned to make disciples from all cultures, but to do that it, too, must be immersed in individual cultures.

No single expression of church can be involved fully with lots of "people groups" simultaneously. Like Christ, the church needs to be culturally specific. "The gospel can only be proclaimed *in* a culture, not *at* a culture"[6] – nor *as* a culture: God's universal word takes root when there is a dialogue between the culture of those who bring it and the culture of those who receive it.

That is why many different expressions of church are emerging. Our society continues to fragment, and the church is taking more varied forms to enter those segments. Single models of church will no longer do. Increasingly, as ministers return from the latest how-to-do-it conference, the model they bring back with them becomes carsick and never makes the journey.

The incarnation brought a change within the Godhead. The Son shrank to a tiny embryo in Mary's womb, and experienced first-hand what it meant to be a human being. Emerging church, likewise, introduces change to the body of Christ. Debut forms of church refashion the body's appearance, as the new is grafted on to the old. As culture changes, so does the church. The process is continuous.

More than candles and cool

Sometimes Christians think of the incarnation as God drawing alongside human beings and identifying with them. But that is just one side of the coin.

The Son did not enter first-century Israel to pat the contemporary culture on its head and say everything was fine. He transformed individuals' lives, and sought to transform society as well – to make it more welcoming to social outcasts, for example, and to replace xenophobia with love for enemies.

So allowing church to be "templated" by its culture need not compromise the gospel. A "mission-shaped church" will be far more than a trendy expression of the latest consumer fad. Taking its cue from the head of the church, turning society inside out will be its goal. The Son of God changed – so that the world would change too. Fresh expressions of church should follow suit.

Sacrifice

If emerging church is to achieve its mission potential, it won't just indulge members who have become disillusioned with the existing church – "Hey, let's do it differently so we can have a more exciting, more authentic time." It will mirror the defining moments of Christ's work – death and resurrection – for the sake of mission.

It hurts!

Emerging church will involve death to preconceived notions of how church should be expressed to create space for new forms of church, suited to the mission context, to emerge. Giving up cherished assumptions about church can be painful.

> In the church I led we planted two congregations, one for families and one for teenagers. Both were in a very different style to what the church was used to. Several long-standing members feared that these new congregations would pull the church away from its "central Anglican" roots. "Dying to live" would mean accepting this change in identity for the sake of mission. It was an extremely painful sacrifice for some to make.

Christians involved in emerging church may have to die to their preferences to live for the preferences of others. Perhaps a group decides to worship twice a month in their preferred style rather than every week, as members would have liked. This frees up two sessions a month to explore the gospel with non-believers. The style and pace of the two sessions are designed for people from outside church: believers' preferences come second.

Fresh expressions of church can be time-consuming, feel like a marathon, be misunderstood by the wider church and prove disappointing – more than their fair share of "Good Fridays", you might think. At times "think pleasure and then double it" can be far from reality.

From his study of emerging Christian groups in South Wales,

Richard Sudworth has this advice: "Take the long view. A constant thread in all these discussions has been the need for churches to invest in the long term as they step out with new forms of mission. The results are not instantaneous and require commitment, patience and the struggle born out of genuineness, not expedience."[7] The expectations of our instant culture may have to be put into the grave so that new styles of church can be successfully resurrected.

Easter on Blackheath

In the mid 1990s, St Michael's Blackheath, in south-east London, appointed Conrad Parsons to develop its work on two local estates where it had little presence. The initial vision seems to have been undergirded by a "come" approach – come to St Michael's and find Christ. But over the years this vision slowly died.

The team of volunteers discovered that suspicion of church was widespread; they realised they were in for a long haul. Relationships were gradually formed, especially with three "gate-keepers" on one of the estates. Members of St Michael's were welcomed on to the committee of Brooklands Park Residents' Association, and increasingly worked in partnership with the residents and to their agenda.

Perhaps the biggest breakthrough came when volunteers from St Michael's joined with local residents to clear a pond that was a major landmark, but had become an eyesore. Huge fun was had by all ages as people turned out to clear the debris. Afterwards people commented, "Before it was them and us. Now it is just us." St Michael's had at last become part of the community. All sorts of opportunities for service now opened up.

A key step was when the Residents' Committee invited Conrad to start church services on the estate. St Michael's church agreed to Conrad's vision of a "Pond church", made up of small groups on the estate. They agreed that a small team from St Michael's would initially resource it, and that Conrad would be released from his remaining commitments at St Michael's. The residents, rather than the culture at St Michael's, would shape the new church. Over three years after Conrad's appointment, the first service was held. One vision had died, but a new one was coming alive.[8]

Reproduction

It is extraordinary that reproduction is instinctive to all forms of life except, it seems, many local churches in the West! When species fail to reproduce, of course, they become extinct – and that danger faces parts of the church today.

Just before returning to heaven, Jesus told his disciples to reproduce what he had done. He had made them disciples, and – echoing his teaching on previous occasions – they were to do the same with "all nations" (Matthew 28:19). One way of reading the two volumes, Luke and Acts, is to see how the life of Christ continued into the life of the early church. The first Christians "reproduced" Jesus.

It's in the genes

Reproduction is fundamental to God's mission. The Spirit seeks to reproduce the Son in believers, who are children of God and drawn into the likeness of Christ. Believers are to reproduce themselves by adding to their number. Many of the parables of the Kingdom concern reproductive growth.

John 15 uses a vine to explore the idea of fruitfulness among the followers of Jesus. The passage contains "an intriguing progression. No fruit vs. 2, fruit vs. 4, much fruit vs. 8, fruit that will last vs. 16. The exponential verse numbers are amusingly coincidental. The key question is: what is fruit for? Certainly it is to be enjoyed and to nourish, but is it a total accident that fruit is the biological mode of reproduction?"[9]

Christians have sought to reproduce themselves by planting new churches. The very first Christians reproduced something of the community life they had enjoyed with Jesus. The church in Jerusalem then reproduced itself throughout the Middle East and into Europe and Asia. St Paul was not content to plant one church: he kept doing it.

"Ephesians 4 lists Christ-given ministries: apostles, prophets, evangelists, pastors/teachers. Although the term has wider meaning, apostles plant churches. Planting establishes the community from which further apostolic, prophetic and evangelistic ministry proceed and which, through pastoring and teaching, grows to maturity in Christ."[10]

A rising birth rate?

Throughout history, into the modern missionary movement and now, for example, on the West's new housing estates, the body of Christ has reproduced itself by planting new churches. Reproduction has been so fundamental to the spread of the church that we take it for granted – and then forget it!

Emerging church is the latest instalment of a long-running story. It seeks not to reproduce clones, just as parents do not naturally reproduce clones of themselves, but congregations that have something of a family likeness and yet also express their own distinctive character. God has built the need for "difference" into the genetics of our world – inbreeding tends to produce malformation (and there has been plenty of that in the church!). Emerging church seeks to reproduce healthily.[11]

Fresh expressions of church will strike gold when they repeat the process – when having been established, they reproduce themselves not as "look-alikes" but as authentic communities in the cultures they aim to serve.

For many this will seem like flying pigs: "if our little group survives, that will be an achievement in itself!" But some church plants have reproduced. Holy Trinity Brompton, a Church of England bastion of church planting, has established 15 plants since 1987. A handful are grandchildren.[12] Will emerging church trump each success by giving birth not just to children, but to grandchildren and even great grandchildren? Mission is never accomplished.

Diversity

Some church leaders say that they are all in favour of new forms of church, but then go on to trumpet a particular genre. They haven't yet travelled to the emerging church mindset. It is time to swat away the simplistic idea that you can replace one model of church with another. Emerging church is not an Ikea flat pack: it's about diversity – encouraging one expression of church here, and a very different one there. The mission context shapes the form.

Different finger prints

Diversity is a hallmark of the Spirit. By indwelling individuals, the Spirit shares their pains and struggles, as well as their joys. The Spirit becomes soaked in each person's unique life. This is paralleled in the Spirit's work among cultural groups. The Spirit leads the church into different cultures.

Pentecost witnessed a dramatic declaration in favour of diversity. The Spirit did not enable the various groups in Jerusalem to speak the same language: the apostles were equipped to speak in different languages. The church had a diversity policy at its inception.

Early Christians quickly translated the gospel out of the language and culture of Jesus, as the church spread to non-Jewish groups. Church practice varied, too – in leadership arrangements, for example, from prophets and teachers (Acts 13:1), to elders (Titus 1:5), to overseers and deacons (1 Timothy 3:1ff.), to plain "leaders" (Hebrews 13:7). Churches have had a multitude of expressions ever since – from a variety of formal and informal liturgies, to different forms of governance, to all sorts of music styles.

Mission has been most effective when diversity has elbowed its way to the table. After Hudson Taylor arrived as a missionary to China in the late 1800s, he wanted his ministry to be different to the "English way". He decided to change everything from his haircut and clothing, to how he spent his time, to his whole approach to mission. His board in England neither understood nor approved. Eventually, Taylor had to start his own missionary board. Church is at its best when it fits people like a glove, not a straitjacket.

Love them in pieces

If we deny diversity, we open the door to domination. When you bring lots of people together, usually the more educated or affluent take control. They make the key decisions and set the tone.

> A church in a working class area began to draw in people from the neighbourhood and grow. Middle-class people heard that it was a "successful" church and started to attend. After a couple of years, some of the original members drifted away. "It doesn't feel the same any more" they complained. Unintentionally, the new arrivals had changed the culture. The less educated no longer felt at home.

In our fallen world, fusing cultures allows the more fortunate to stifle other people. The under-confident have less scope to flourish and express their gifts. A study of urban regeneration projects concluded, "If the community is seen as homogeneous then only the most powerful voices will tend to be heard."[13]

Often love requires that groups keep their separate identities. Cultural fragmentation can be turned into a force for liberation. Perhaps that's why, in George Carey's telling phrase, the Holy Spirit never leaves identical fingerprints – either on individuals or on Christian communities. The Spirit wants groups to be set free.

The way to encourage emerging church is not to teach a particular model – "base communities" or cell church, for instance. Emerging church is not a model, it is a prism. Churches need a different way of seeing, not a new method. So throw away your old specs: 20:20 vision will bring diversity into view.

Is theodiversity as important as biodiversity?

Should we celebrate variety over truth? Brian McLaren, an emerging church commentator in the United States, told *Christianity+Renewal* magazine, "Jesus never led anyone in the sinner's prayer, he never invited anyone to accept him as his personal Lord and Saviour. No one ever 'got saved', or had 'a born again experience' – these are modern ways of describing Christianity. We are fooling ourselves if we say the message never changes.'[14]

Many in emerging church would agree. Not only is the form of church up for grabs, but how we understand the gospel too. No one reads the Bible with a clean mental slate. We always bring to the text the influences of our culture, our families and our personalities. These shape how we interpret what we read.

Many of our understandings of the gospel have been framed by the last 200 years – by "modern" rationalist values, which are now being challenged by the "postmodern" mood. We need to rediscover the authentic gospel, claim some advocates of emerging church. Christian thought has never stood still. Each generation has found new aspects of God's truth. Our generation must do the same.

Brian McLaren calls on the church to "de-bug its faith from the viruses of modernity" – the control virus, the mechanistic virus, the reductionist virus, the secular/scientific virus, the virus of individualism, the organisational virus and the consumerist virus.[15] Emerging church includes emerging truth.

Not everyone in fresh expressions of church would go that far. Many prefer to drape a conservative theology over their initiatives. They want to retain their inherited understanding of truth. Reshaped church, they think, will provide an easier-to-open container for traditional beliefs – a changing church with an unchanging gospel.

Stuart Murray Williams writes:

At present, too many emerging churches are culturally creative but theologically conservative. Tinkering with shape, style and structure represents only superficial change. New ways of interpreting the Bible and new theological insights will be needed if new ways of being church are to have lasting missiological significance.

It may be important not to identify emerging church with one side of this debate. Emerging church welcomes all sorts under its umbrella. Radicals or conservatives should beware of coralling the term and claiming "Emerging Church R Us". As the wheat-and-tares parable makes clear, God is the ultimate judge of theological correctness. Perhaps the greatest truth is "All will know that you are my disciples if you love one another" (John 13:35).

> **George Lings writes:**
> *My take on this is that it is the* essence *of both Gospel and Church that remains constant. Both then have to be re-expressed in ways that the culture to which God sends us can understand. Even in the New Testament the very words, gospel and church, were borrowed, secular terms. That's what gave them meaning.*

Unity

Naysayers go into overdrive at the idea of "catalogue church" – you flip through the pages and pick what you fancy. Doesn't this baptise choice at the expense of commitment to the rest of Christ's body?

But the New Testament balances diversity with unity. Jesus prayed that his followers would be one (John 17:11). The epistles constantly warn against disunity. St Paul urged his new congregations to help the church in Jerusalem, which faced poverty (2 Corinthians 8). Cultural diversity was to be matched by reconciliation and mutual involvement.

Falling apart?

Revelation 21 pictures the time when humanity is gathered together in a perfect civilisation, "the new Jerusalem". Verse 24 imagines "the kings of the earth" bringing all "their splendour" into the city. Verse 26 repeats the idea: "The glory and honour of the nations will be brought into it." Choice pickings from each civilisation will be brought together in a bright alchemy of human achievement.

Diversity is affirmed – "kings" and "nations" are referred to in the plural. But the accomplishments of the different nations are assembled in one place. Unity is not dull uniformity. Cultures dazzle and enrich each other as they stand side by side.

"The gospel is not a statement about some remote future; it is the dawn of that future . . ."[16] The church is to model God's future for humanity, pointing men and women towards the hope that lies ahead. Specifically, in a society that seems to be pulling apart, church is to live the day when cultural fragments will be meshed together. Diversity is not the last word. It is written alongside oneness and reconciliation.

Rainbow church

So as emerging church, chameleon-like, changes colour according to its context, it will look for ways of blending the colours together. It will put as much stress on unity as diversity. All sorts of possibilities exist for joining different Christians together, from short evening courses, to weekend retreats, to social events, to pilgrimages and holidays.

Cheriton Baptist Church in Folkestone, south east England, has a children's gathering, a teenage gathering and an adult gathering, with the possibility of a further gathering for the twenties age group.

The existing three gatherings meet separately on Sunday mornings twice a month, but on the other two Sundays they come together. At these joint meetings children, teenagers or adults may lead the first part of the service. Then the age groups separate into their distinct gatherings for the teaching slot.

On alternate months, the gatherings study the same theme or Bible passage on each Sunday of the month. The aim is to strengthen family life by encouraging households to talk about what they have been learning. Each age group is also encouraged to serve the whole

church in some way. Older teenagers, for instance, are invited to lead some of the children's work under the supervision of an adult. Diversity is affirmed, but the different ages are threaded together.

Stuart Murray Williams writes:

Is it enough to encourage different groups to "inter-mix"? If emerging churches are going to be more diverse than ever before, surely more than inter-mixing will be needed to balance glorious diversity with deep and meaningful unity? This is one of the major challenges facing the diversifying church – how to embody both unity and diversity in radical and liberating ways.

A values statement?

Emerging church reveals – or has the potential to reveal – seven "faces" of God: the God who is interdependent, who builds experiments into creation, who seeks to transform creation, who died and rose to make transformation possible, who uses reproduction to help bring about transformation, who reproduces not clones but a diversity of forms, and who prizes unity alongside diversity.

Might a group that is planning a fresh expression of church build these values into its mission statement – interdependence between the new and existing church, experimentation, transformation as the goal, sacrifice for the sake of mission, reproduction by each generation of emerging church, diversity and unity?[17] Perhaps these are values that a congregation can explore together, as it considers whether to launch a new kind of church.

Emerging church is more than a pragmatic response to declining numbers: it is a theological vision – a wide-eyed vision that escapes a blinkered past, challenges the church status quo, and calls forth new forms of community in which individuals can encounter Christ authentically. Might these communities renew inherited congregations and become the crucible of church in the "postmodern" world?

Notes

1. Dan Kimball, *The Emerging Church,* Grand Rapids: Zondervan, 2003, p. 92.
2. Graham Cray, *Youth Congregations and the Emerging Church*, Cambridge: Grove Books, 2002, p. 22.
3. 1 Corinthians 15:24.
4. www.nccc.org.au/files/nccc/Exploring.
5. The idea of God as a learner raises some knotty theological questions, which are well answered by John M. Hull, *What Prevents Christian Adults from Learning?*, London: SCM, 1985, Chapter Five.
6. *Mission-shaped Church*, London: Church House Publishing, 2004, p. 87.
7. www.emergingchurch.info/reflection/richardsudworth/principles.
8. George Lings, "'Across the Pond'," *Encounters on the Edge*, No. 6, Church Army: The Sheffield Centre, 2000. The church plant subsequently fell on hard times – see Chapter Seven.
9. George Lings, "Anglican Church Plants, Church Structures, Church Doctrine, Their Relationships", A sabbatical report, 1992, p. 113.
10. *Mission-shaped Church*, op. cit., p. 95.
11. I am grateful to David Muir for pointing this out.
12. George Lings and Stuart Murray, *Church Planting: Past, Present and Future*, Cambridge: Grove Books, 2003, p. 22.
13. "Community participants perspectives on involvement in area regeneration programmes", *Findings*, Joseph Rowntree Foundation, July 2000.
14. Quoted by Andy Peck in "A beginner's guide to Emerging Church", *Christianity+Renewal*, January 2004, p. 14.
15. Brian D. McLaren, *The Church on the Other Side*, Grand Rapids: Zondervan, 2000, pp. 189–97.
16. Jurgen Moltmann, *The Church in the Power of the Spirit*, London: SCM, 1977, p. 77.

17. These values are not the only possibilities: an alternative set could be derived from the Anglican publication, *Mission-shaped Church*, op. cit., pp. 81–2.

CHAPTER THREE

NEW WORLD, NEW CHURCH

Now is the "chairos", alarm clock moment to experiment with the church. Many existing congregations are "dead church walking". Yet mission doors to the consumer world are swinging open. Only new types of church will be invited in. Experiments in Christian community are needed urgently. They will reveal what types of church will gain entry to the spend, spend society.

Church is fading

In the early 1990s there were 24,000 14- to 24-year-olds in the greater Watford area: a mere 700 had any contact with church.[1] A few years later, a Huddersfield survey discovered that an astonishing 58% of adults claimed *never* to have been in church.[2]

The freefall in church attendance is a siren to slay complacency. Table 3.1 paints a grim picture for the 1980s and 1990s. More recent years haven't been much better. Peter Brierley reckons that by 2005, Sunday attendance in English churches could have plummeted from 7.5% of the population in 1998 to 6.7%.[3] The Great Church Decline is well advanced.

Table 3.1. Church attendance in England is falling

Year	% population attending on average Sunday (%)
1979	11.7
1989	9.9
1998	7.5

Source: Peter Brierley, *The Tide is Running Out*, Eltham: Christian Research, 2000, p. 27.

Panic button?

Almost a half of all churchgoers in England are over 45; a quarter are over 65 (see Table 3.2). If more young people don't attend, churches will continue to empty simply because older people are passing away.

Table 3.2. The Church is Top-heavy: church attendance in England, 1998

Age group	Number	% churchgoers
15–29	537,200	15
30–44	646,700	17
45–64	885,500	24
65+	927,900	25

Source: Peter Brierley, *The Tide is Running Out*, p. 93.

Attendance could be kept stable – but not grow – if the same number of younger people came into church as older people flowed out. Yet this seems most unlikely. Sunday attendance in the UK by children under 15 is headed in exactly the wrong direction. Table 3.3 shows that the total halved in the 1980s and 1990s.

Table 3.3. The church is haemorrhaging children: church attendance by the under 15s, 1979–98.

Year	Number
1979	1,416,000
1989	1,177,000
1998	717,100

Source: Peter Brierley, *The Tide is Running Out*, p. 94.

Only a tiny proportion of children are now in the UK church. The figure is down from 35% in 1940 to 14% in 1970 and just 6% in 2000. That means that 94% of young people are not in church on Sunday. No wonder this has been described as a "time bomb".[4]

> *Stuart Murray Williams writes:*
> *Many ethnic churches are shining exceptions to the story of decline. The critical mission issue they face is whether and how they can break out of their own communities and effectively evangelise and disciple people from other ethnic groups. Many African leaders in London, for instance, are acutely aware of this challenge, committed to doing this but struggling to know what to do.*

Does the shrivelling up of church matter? Some Christians would say it is a question literally of life and death: individuals' place in heaven is at stake. Others would say that the health of society depends partly on the health of the church – if you go to church you are more likely to do voluntary work and have altruistic values.[5] Others again would say that in our polarised and polluted world the gospel call to transform society has never been more urgent. Whatever view you take, pulling the plug on church should cause alarm.

Why is church failing?

Historian Callum Brown has declared, "Britain is showing the world how religion as we have known it can die."[6] Sociologist Steve Bruce, piling statistic on statistic, argues that not only the church, but "God is dead".[7] Struggling congregations in villages, outer estates and increasingly the suburbs smell the stench of decay. Churchgoers are in a failing organisation – and it hurts. Why has the church been doing so badly?

The urban struggle

One reason is that the "party-on" society has left poor people behind. In its wake are tatty buildings, brutally graffitied pavements and stairwells, tower blocks with broken lifts, and upturned rubbish bags that provide food for stray dogs. In particular, the forces that have propelled consumerism have also destroyed community in many inner cities and outer estates.

A single mother who treks half an hour to the shops because there's no transport, who wages guerrilla war with the father of her new child, who is up several times in the night and who is constantly worried about money will be too exhausted to give church a thought. If she thinks about it at all, she will probably imagine that religion is another set of duties, when she is burdened enough already.

If a nearby church provided community, she might find the support, belonging and affirmation that would make life more bearable. Yet despite wonderful exceptions, many churches in poor Britain find it extraordinarily hard to be community. Complex and deep-seated processes, decades long, are largely to blame.

People with ability and resourcefulness have moved to more affluent areas, denuding the urban poor of potential leaders. Waves of immigration in the 1950s and 1960s brought in newcomers who were shunned by the existing churches and who set up their own, or who had different faiths and were uninterested in church. Local communities began to fragment.

Slum clearance bulldozed many inhabitants from inner cities to new outer estates, where the incomers felt uprooted and forgotten, and where all the deprivation of inner cities returned.

The closure of many traditional industries in the 1980s and early 1990s gave a cruel twist to the story. Unemployment wreaked havoc on families. Teenage girls saw motherhood rather than work as a route to adult life. Crime became a more lucrative source of income than employment. Drugs blocked out despair and bred disorder. Though some local economies have turned round, others remain savagely scarred.

These circumstances, so often described,[8] make it exception-ally difficult for church to be community, to support poor people and to create pathways into faith. Ordained and lay leaders have been run ragged, often with little support.

Despite the obstacles, some churches have knit local people together – with services in Swahili or Spanish, effective commu-nity programmes and a strong presence in the schools, for example. Others have become hermits in their old age – hidden behind grey buildings, unrepresentative of the local scene and on the verge of a complete wipe out.

Paul Thomson, who helped establish the RAVEN post-club project in Edinburgh, has described how – remarkably – he and about 40 of his friends, as teenagers, found Christ on their Aberdeen housing estate during the late 1970s.

No one ever told us about this incredible strange figure in that strange big book. We stumbled on to him – it was OUR delicious secret, like finding ET in your kitchen, at the backside of the world. The estate was a terrifying place. Many of us were beaten every week . . . Some of our chums – both boys and girls – were currently being abused by dads [and] uncles . . .

We would gather together every day. We'd pack our ma's place, when she was at "yoga", 40 of us, some on "glue", bringing ghetto-blasters, biscuits, pocket-money – to put in bowls to share – [and] we'd fill every room – kitchen, bedrooms, sitting room, hallway, outside in the backyard. When one of us said, "They're starting tae speak to God in the sitting room", everyone would squeeze in or join in thru the hatch . . . I remember that it gave us "guys" permis-sion to talk, really talk to each other. We even had a game. We would give each other all our wages (part-time jobs) at the end of the week, or lay hands on our dog to see what would happen . . .

One day a man heard about us . . . visited us and was blown away. He started using words like "revival" etc. . . . He advised us to start "going to church". Very soon, though, it died. They didn't mean for it to, it just did. I now understand that whatever lived in that soil or environment was too fragile to be moved into an alien landscape. I remember watching it, the uprooted crew at church. Slowly they got quieter, less animated, less free and themselves. Our language made people wince, our route into Christianity completely alien.[9]

On many estates, the huge gulf between life and church that Paul experienced has now become a gigantic canyon.

Hyper choice

For the bulk of the population, those outside the inner cities and outer estates, the story of church decline is very different. Consumerism has brought mega choice, which has revolutionised their lives. Before the Second World War, individuals were largely shaped by their social and family backgrounds, and the places where they were brought up. Your upbringing determined the rest of your life.

During the 1950s mass consumption spread across Europe and expanded consumer choice phenomenally. A supermarket in the late 1960s had around 2,000 product lines. A medium-sized one today has around 22,000 and a hypermarket 40,000. As consumer choice exploded, individuals were increasingly "unboxed" from their backgrounds.

Some went to university where they were exposed to alternative lifestyles. Others saw alternative lifestyles on television. Slowly they could afford to buy these alternative lifestyles. People's lives were less determined by their upbringing, and more by the choices they made as consumers.

This had a particular impact on women. Callum Brown argues that well before the late 1950s men had begun to attend church less regularly, if at all. But they still associated with the church; they had their children baptised and attended the major festivals. What kept them plugged in was the continuing commitment of their wives.

Since the late 1950s, however, women have become steadily detached from the church. They went out to work to produce consumer goods on the one hand and generate the income to buy them on the other. They had less time for their local communities, including the church.

More important perhaps, their identity changed. No longer did they view themselves as stay-at-home wives and full-time mothers, but as working women. Their views about marriage shifted. Paid work gave them the financial independence to leave their husbands, if they chose.

The hammer blow was the sexual revolution. Though this was made possible by the pill, it was egged on (one might add) by the ethic of choice and pleasure intrinsic to mass consumption. Sexual freedom knocked traditional ideas of family stone dead. Teenage girls came to have a radically different view of their place in the world. They didn't expect to live in an inherited mould: they would shape their own lives, thank you, through choice.

Yet much of the church still assumed the moral tramlines that younger women were leaving – the "traditional" family where no one had sex before they were married, the wife was at home, the husband at work and they lived happily together for life. By the time the church had begun to change, these women were taking it for granted that Christianity was irrelevant. They became unglued from the church, detaching their husbands and children too.[10]

Central to consumerism has been the ethic of choice – "it's up to you", "be your own person" or as a clothing company advertised, "think for yourself". Choice, Steve Bruce argues, undermines faith. If "it's your decision", clearly you won't feel bound by an external authority. You will feel free to ignore it, which is bad news for religion that is based on authority. The freedom to choose competes with the power of community. If "it's up to you", you will ignore the group when it suits you.

Once authority and community are undermined, commitment to faith is weakened. Individuals will not make sacrifices because of God, or because they have been taught to do so by the church or because of loyalty to the group. It becomes harder for something other than self-interest to take priority.

Our user-chooser culture dilutes the motivation for evangelism. Allowing people to think for themselves becomes more important than getting everyone to think the same. Bruce argues that consumerism threatens the church with nuclear grief.[11]

Left behind

For most people church is on a different page. It doesn't intrude on their lives. When crises strike they turn to friends, doctors or counsellors, but never dream of church. Is night closing in on Christianity? The case for mission could hardly be more pressing.

The church will never make up the ground it has lost to consumerism by keeping its distance from consumerism. Only by taking seriously the culture of choice will the church have a future.

When people think "it's up to you", the church won't get away with being dogmatic and hierarchical: it needs to be more like a partner, working with individuals as they explore belief for themselves – "this is how the passage has often been understood, but how do you read it?" (Time to farewell the traditional sermon?) Here's a way for the church to imitate the partnering role of the Spirit in believers' lives.

In a society that prizes the choice, church will be isolated if it treats everyone the same. A local church offering one-size-fits-all will deny choice to those who don't fit, and be ignored. A congregation that dresses worshippers in a straitjacket ("all stand for the next song") will feel alien, and be sidelined. Can the church learn to be more consumer-shaped without losing its God shape?

The challenge is urgent. In some areas of deprivation the church is almost extinct. Mission among the urban poor often relies on individuals who are better off – as a source of income, as volunteers sometimes (witness Manchester's Eden Project), and as citizens who may vote with excluded people in mind. If suburban churches stare into the abyss, what hope will exist for the urban church? Connecting to the consumer world is vital for mission to poor and rich people alike.

Experiments are vital to discover how the church can make

these connections. But is consumerism so vicious that the church does not stand a chance? Has the spiritual terrain become so barren that the church is bound to wither away? Or are new opportunities arriving for mission? Might emerging church prove Brown, Bruce and other "gloom gluttons" wrong?

A doomed church?

"We are all consumers now." Consumer behaviour has run down the income ladder. A cleaner in Britain today could well holiday overseas. In a must-read for the new century, Shoshana Zuboff and James Maxmin comment, "In an advanced industrial society, consumption is a necessity, not a luxury. It is what people must do to survive. It's the way that individuals take care of themselves and their families . . . Everyone is a consumer, no matter what their status or income level."[12]

Consumerism is even changing how we define poverty. The British Government proposes to classify children as poor if their parents cannot afford to buy them a bicycle, take them swimming at least once a month or invite their school friends round for tea every fortnight.[13] This reflects changes in living standards. In 1983, for example, only 32% of people thought that having friends or family visit for a meal was a necessity. By 1999, this had risen to 65%.[14]

Higher living standards will continue to dig in consumerism. An unambitious view of the future would expect average real incomes to grow roughly as fast as in the past three decades. Living standards would be around 60% higher in 20 years and would have doubled within 28 years.[15] Many of today's consumer dreams would be within reach of people on even the most modest incomes. Living standards in 2025 Liverpool may approach London in 2005.[16] Engaging with consumers will be a task for the church throughout society, not just in affluent areas.

Spiritual spending

Much consumer spending – or the desire to spend – has a spiritual dimension. It reflects longings that can also be met in individuals' spiritual lives, and this will persist.

Buying a lifestyle, for example, expresses the search for identity. Looking good – through clothes, cosmetics and all the rest – reflects the desire to be accepted. Eating out with friends is a way to belong. An Internet chat-room may help you feel connected to a bigger whole. Looking forward to a holiday may give meaning to a boring job.

Identity, acceptance, belonging, connection to the whole and meaning – these are the stuff of faith, the genome of Christianity. The continued demand for them will create openings for the church. Can the church welcome these opportunities, while critiquing the excesses of consumerism at the same time?

Sometimes church leaders semaphore a negative message. They give the impression that Christianity is against what individuals enjoy in their everyday lives. Many people conclude that the church has little to contribute to their deepest longings – to their search for identity, acceptance and ways of achieving their other aspirations. They don't see the church as being on their side. In its attempt to be prophetic, the church undermines its mission.

Consumer desires should not be things for the church to battle against, but entry-points for the gospel – opportunities for the church to connect with people and be a channel of grace.

George Lings writes:

I hope Mike will develop this. How to be counter-cultural from within the consumerist culture is our biggest challenge, not least because its values have eaten so deeply into the existing church. One way might be to say, "Discipleship is a life of choice – life or death at its most stark. How then can we learn to choose what not *to have? How can we fashion communities of those we choose not to exclude? What messages from the culture do we choose to debunk? What positive alternatives and consequences can we live out?"*

The experience economy[17]

Our society has entered the "experience economy". American management gurus, Joseph Pine and James Gilmour, have described how consumers have been boring themselves to death.[18] They go to the same old shopping malls, see the same old shops, view the same old brands and they long for something new, something exciting, something that will arrest their attention.

This has created an appetite for experiences, which retailers and manufacturers are hurrying to meet. Many restaurants, for example, see their prime activity as providing a particular experience of eating, rather than just selling food. Food becomes a prop for what is known as "eatertainment". Shopping itself is being transformed into an experience, with sights that titillate the eyes, subtle aromas and background music to produce the right ambience.

Writing for a business audience, Pine and Gilmour asked: What type of experiences will consumers want in the years ahead? Their reply? Life-transforming experiences.

Growing numbers of people seek experiences that will transform them in some way. If they are reasonably well off, they go to the gym and punish themselves for an hour to look better. Or they acquire new skills to become successful and more interesting people. Or they study the culture of their holiday destination to become better informed.

Self-improvement is a defining feature of our age. People want to be transformed so that they become better. And that of course is the business of the church – to help individuals have life-transforming experiences of God that lead to self-improvement. Can the church meet consumers at this point of desire?

The thirst for experience may partly explain the widespread interest in "spirituality". A local FE college offers classes in Aromatherapy, Astrology, Crystal Healing, Indian Head Massage, Reiki, Tai Chi and the list keeps growing. Why not Christian Meditation as well? A chaplain in Bath wanted to run an evening class on spirituality, as a way into the Christian faith, but had to prop up the existing church instead. Another minister, in Lincolnshire, has started a spiritual keep-fit class.

Church members meeting in a David Lloyd leisure centre have asked whether they should start "spiritual aerobics". (Some Buddhist groups do this.) Each session would end with a period of silence for people to encounter God "as they understand him" or simply to get in touch with their feelings. Hurry, hurry people need the headspace. In due course, individuals might be encouraged to share their experiences and any answers to prayer. If some wanted to explore this further, they could meet at a separate time. They might plunder ideas from *Essence*, a Christian course on spirituality that assumes no prior Christian knowledge.[19] Perhaps this could lead to *Alpha*, and even – possibly – to a new, if small, expression of church.

Liquid lives

People's lives are a bit like a box, in which lines used to be drawn horizontally. In the past people left school at the age of 16, married in their early twenties, had children a few years later and retired at the age of 60 or 65.

For many people, the lines are now being redrawn – vertically. Learning continues all through your life. People often cohabit, marry, separate, cohabit and marry again. Individuals have children in their late twenties and thirties, and may become parents again in their late forties and fifties. The retirement age is becoming more flexible, and will be even more so in the future. More and more people are living liquid lives.

At the same time, they are expecting more from each phase of their lives. The focus for most people has shifted away from material necessities like housing, food and clothes. Individuals take these for granted. The search is now on for emotional satisfaction.

Food becomes an opportunity to have fun with friends. Clothes help you connect with the right sort of people. In marriage, the emphasis is on companionship and a satisfying emotional life. Expectations of retirement are rising – adventure holidays, new hobbies and even hang-gliding!

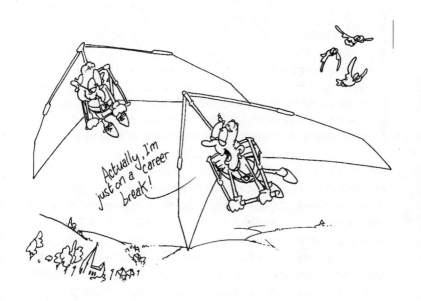

Of course, not everyone has these opportunities. But as our society becomes more affluent, rising expectations will ripple out to people on the edge.[20] Individuals will seek to express themselves more fully at each stage of life.

More fluid transitions means more choice, which increases the possibility that individuals will make the wrong choice. Higher expectations mean that there is more at stake. Put the two together and not surprisingly decisions feel risky. "Will it be the right option?" "Is it the best choice?" "Will I achieve my hopes?"

To minimise these risks, individuals are turning to experts to help them choose and get the most out of life – mentors, coaches, parenting courses, dating agencies (with psychological profiling to match couples), consultants to help them select the colour scheme for their new homes, fitness advisers and many more. The demand for choice-busting "life managers" will continue to grow.[21] This will present huge opportunities to the church.

In particular, parenting courses will continue to mushroom. A recent study for the Department for Education and Science has caused a stir. It confirmed what most teachers already know – that variations in the quality of parenting have a bigger impact on learning outcomes than differences between schools. Interventions to improve parenting can be highly effective.[22] Civil servants are said to be asking, "Why do we keep upping the spending on schools, when the home is even more vital?"

Might Government pour larger sums into parenting courses? In which case, who will run them? There could be big openings for churches with enterprise.

One lay leader in Wakefield runs a mums-and-tots group. Her vision is to offer the mothers a parenting course, which might then lead to a series on "Questions children ask", which might be followed by sessions on "Questions adults ask", which might give rise to "Spiritual resources that can help us at home". The next stage might be a course introducing Christianity, followed by the *Emmaus* course,

> which has a stronger discipleship element. By the end, if people stayed, she would effectively have a small worshipping congregation. Her aim would not be to encourage them to attend church, but to build church around the community that had formed.

Relational recreation

Still more than in the past, relationships will be at the heart of leisure. This jars with the claim that society is becoming more atomistic. American sociologist Robert Putnam, for example, has argued that Americans have become increasingly disconnected from family, friends, neighbours and social groupings such as church, recreational clubs and political parties. People prefer chat shows on television to chatting with each other.[23]

Some people think that the same is happening in Britain. The number of people living on their own, for instance, is projected to rise from under a fifth of all households in 1971 to approaching two-fifths in 2016 – a sign, it is suggested, of individuals becoming more isolated.[24]

But there is evidence against Putnam and others, some of it quite surprising. For example, between 1961 and 1995 the average time spent listening to the radio or watching television – as one's main activity – actually fell slightly, from 139 minutes a day to 129. Eating out, drinking in the pub or going to the cinema more than doubled, from a little under half an hour to just over an hour.[25]

Relationships are at the heart of consumer behaviour. People eat and drink together. They like to watch sport – together. How many people go to the cinema on their own? Individuals select clothes and cosmetics that help them relate to their peers.

Relationships are central even to the weekly shop. The mother – and usually it is the mother – asks herself, "What do others in the family like?" "What's best for them?" Shopping becomes an act of love. Daniel Miller, a social anthropologist, has even described it as "making love in the supermarket".[26]

Relationships are not dying, they are changing. Quite recently, one of my students returned from two years in China.

I asked him what had struck him on his return. He replied, "In China they relate to each other through the family. They talk about the family and they do things as families." He was taken aback when people asked, "What do your grandparents think about you coming to China?"

"In England," he continued, "it's so different. People relate to each other through consumerism. We talk about the films we have seen, the soaps we have watched on television or the latest advert. If we want to do something with a friend, typically it is some form of consumer activity." Consumerism is the medium for relationships.

Again, this creates opportunities for the church. Relationships are at the core of church, and there is a hunger for them. In a recent book, Martin Robinson and Dwight Smith cite unpublished research,

> which attempted to discover the values of younger people outside the church. Derek Hughes was struck by the extent to which young people longed to be loved, to have authentic relationships, to experience meaningful community. In fact they tended to describe their longings in precisely the terms that the New Testament describes the true nature of the church. Significantly, when asked, "What would you give to be part of such a community?" they responded, "Almost anything."[27]

That is one reason why people are experimenting with café-style church and cell expressions of church. Many people find them more relational than traditional congregations.

A failed fix?

Yet consumerism leaves a hole in many people's lives, "a dark side to the American dream". Two marketing experts have written, "For the first time in human history, a shared mythos has broken down, and commercial messages are now taking the place of shared sacred stories. We know in our hearts that a profession designed to sell products cannot fill this gap. If we take the time to think of how many people are finding the only meaning they have in their lives from consumption of various sorts, we do not feel proud; we feel sad, or even outraged."[28]

Consumerism fails to satisfy because experiences wear off. "Is that all there is to life? Is it round the buoy again?" Other people can buy more or better products than you can. There is always something you can't have: you love the three-star hotel, but wonder what it is like in four-star.

Consumer spending involves choice, which – as we have seen – creates anxiety. "Am I getting the best deal?" "Would I do better by spending the money on something else?" Choosing one thing means that you have to reject the alternative, something that you might have wanted. Choice can be tinged with disappointment.[29]

Many people will be looking for more in the years ahead. How will the church respond? Marketers tell companies that their products need "unique selling points". That is also true for the church if it wants to engage with the consumer culture. The church will never connect with the thirst for experiences, the demand for life managers and the voracious appetite for relationships unless it can add something special.

Why would someone go to a café church rather than Starbucks, unless the former had extra to offer? Why go to "spiritual aerobics" unless real value is added by the spiritual add-on? Why attend a Christian parenting course unless the faith element provides distinctive support?

Nick Spencer of the London Institute for Contemporary Christianity has been researching non-churchgoers' attitudes to life and faith for the Church of England's Diocese of Coventry. No matter how atheistic or materialistic ('we are just bodies that die"), people still have big questions about reality: Why am I here? Where am I going? What's wrong with the world? Does God exist? How should I live my life?

There is massive potential for a church that picks up these questions. The trouble is that people don't naturally turn to church for the answers. The church package is too alien –

church is seen as being about "church things" rather than "life things". Can the church help individuals to explore the answers in ways that connect with their everyday lives?

Two marketers from a business school recently berated me: "The church is setting its standards too low!" They don't go to church themselves, but they argued that from a marketing perspective the church needed to stick to the moral and spiritual high ground. "If you don't, you will have nothing unique to offer the world."

A church with more?

For too long, the church has suffered from attention deficit disorder with regard to opportunities in the consumer world. Spiritual spending, the experience economy, liquid lives, relational recreation, a failed fix – all these create openings for mission. Will Christians grasp these opportunities? If they do, what types of mission-sculpted church will they require?

Traditional church

First, traditional church, today's church, will still have currency. Traditional communities – geographical communities in which people spend the bulk of their lives – remain widespread. They include many working-class areas and some of the ethnic communities, which hang on to their traditions and are often close-knit.

Not everyone who comes to faith looks for a new expression of church. Many are content with the old. "Postmodern" people often live mosaic lives, pasting snippets from the hyper-modern alongside the traditional. The inherited church may be one of those snippets. Anglican cathedrals have some of the fastest growing congregations in Britain.

Rooted church

Second, "rooted" churches will have a great future. These will be churches that are even more local than the local church.

Some people think that globalisation will make local communities less important to people, that it's obliterating the local. But the opposite is likely. As the world feels increasingly complex and out of control, and as travel looms larger in people's jobs, place will matter even more than it does today. In an unstable world, place will be where you put down roots. Commentators speak about "glocalisation" – the reassertion of the local within the globalisation process.[30]

People certainly travel more, but they are also staying put. A Gallup poll found that 14% of people had moved home in 1952. Half a century later, just 10% of households had shifted in the previous year.[31] The figures are not strictly comparable, but they certainly do not suggest that Britain is becoming a nation of house movers.

Amazingly, according to the RAC Foundation, the number of households relocating in Britain because of jobs halved between 1984 and 1994.[32] When both partners work, more couples are saying, "Let's not move every time one of us changes jobs. We'll make a base here, and if our jobs alter we'll commute the extra distance."

Around half the adult population see their mothers at least once a week, and about two-fifths see their fathers weekly or more. Almost half of all adults live within 30 minutes' journey of their mothers.[33] "Relocation, Relocation" is no more than a television programme.

Place matters to people. As they stay in an area, they slowly get to know their neighbours. Some become friends. Individuals may "talk to the world" by email, but they also connect with people round about. Not all networks are divorced from geography, which creates opportunities for the church in local communities.

However, these communities are fragmenting. Ethnic groups, for example, have enriched many areas and added to the diversity. The number of households in Britain has increased by almost a third over the past 30 years, creating a demand for new homes.[34] The number will grow further in the next two decades, perhaps by a quarter in England (equivalent to the size of greater London).[35] New housing estates tend to attract people with similar lifestyles. Not infrequently, these lifestyles differ to others nearby, fracturing the locality.

The local church may need to think in terms not of a single local community, as in the past, but of different communities – a pastiche of housing estates, ethnic groups, lifestyle communities and people of various ages. Residents may identify more strongly with their particular group than with the village, the town or the suburb. The local church may have to become even more local than in the past. New forms of local will require new forms of local church.

Often, emerging church is thought to equal network church, but that is not always the case. The relationship between networks and geography is too complex. Many people have both dispersed networks and local ones, or want local roots. They may welcome a church that has a neighbourhood presence.

"Rooted church" won't start by asking, "How can we get people from different parts of the area into our one congregation?" Its first questions will be, "What are the various cultures here?" "Are there particular groups that we can serve, perhaps adding spiritual value in the process – parents for example, homeless people, addicts or a new housing estate?" "What would some of us have to do to draw alongside these groups and be welcomed by them?"

Only when a church has become immersed in some of its surrounding fragments will it ask, "Can we help to join these fragments together from time to time?"

George Lings writes:
If a significant number of church leaders reading this book could get these questions asked, and heard, then a major change might occur. Here is all the difference between come-and-go mentality, and between intentional humble diversity and self-satisfied deluded monopoly.

A Baptist church in Daventry is releasing small groups of Christians across the town. Each group is spending time and energy discovering what it means to embody the grace of God for their estate. "This may involve sacrifice and 'dying' to what is comfortable for us – but that is what being the body of Christ is all about . . ."

"In some ways" Graham Old the pastor comments, "it feels like we are somewhere between a church with house groups and a group of house churches. . . . The thing that excites me so far is seeing people who have given up on church deciding to give it a second go."

Convenience stores rather than an ecclesiastical Wal-Mart? Three words that *don't* describe their attitude to being church are: "buildings", "one-size-fits-all" and "out-dated".[36]

Brand church

Third, brand churches could have a promising future. These will be churches that self-consciously brand themselves to reach a particular network.

As choice has expanded, brands have shot up the cultural mast. Brands are much more than a product. They are a collection of associations and symbols that give a product meaning. In a choice-fatigue age, brands help consumers navigate through all the myriad options available. If Ted Baker is your label, there is no need to compare with other makes. When you need a new shirt, you know exactly where to go.

Brands help people to choose by telling a story with strong appeal. Strategic adviser to over 100 international companies and organisations, Rolf Jensen has argued that the story behind the product will increasingly provide business with a competitive edge. The company with the best story will win. In an influential book, Jensen has described some of the stories that will appeal to consumers in the years ahead – for example, "adventures for sale", "care", "togetherness, friendship and love", "who am I?", "peace of mind" and "convictions".[37]

Great opportunities exist for churches that do not focus on a locality, but define themselves precisely to reach a specific group from wider afield. Some of these brand churches will score because of their size, which will enable them to deliver a high standard of music, children's work and teaching courses, for instance. Others will be niche brands, chiselled into a tiny segment of the market.

Vineyard, New Wine churches, Holy Trinity Brompton and Reform churches are just some examples, from the evangelical tradition, of brand churches that have begun to emerge. Each delivers more than an ecclesiastical "product": they have clearly defined values that begin to tell a tale. Individuals attend at least partly because they identify with their church's particular story of the Christian faith.

By and large these churches appeal to specific groups of Christians or lapsed Christians. What we don't see yet, on any scale, are brand churches that appeal strongly to people with no Christian background. Will churches brand themselves for identified groups of non-churchgoers? And will these churches become important features of the mission "brandscape"?

> One middle-class congregation in Cheshire is asking whether it should be branded "Care for the Family". It might strengthen its focus on family life, offer more in the way of parenting courses, develop grandparenting and mentoring roles in relation to youth and young adults, and perhaps campaign for family-friendly local and national policies.
>
> In contrast, one of the new clusters within the St Thomas Crookes network in Sheffield based its expression of church on the cartoon series, "Wacky Races". Members chose this brand because they were into it themselves and they hoped it would appeal to their non-believing friends.

Liquid church

Society is entering a new phase in which a fourth type of church may flourish – what Pete Ward, former youth adviser to the Archbishop of Canterbury, has described as "liquid church".[38] This is a much more fluid expression of church.

It partly reflects the more personalised way in which organisations are relating to individuals. Even the public services, we're told, are to be personalised – such as hospital appointments at times that suit the patient (most people would be glad to get a hospital appointment at all!).[39] As more and more organisations seek to fit individuals exactly, people's expectations are changing. We have entered an it-must-fit-me world.[40]

This is coinciding with the mobile phone revolution. Individuals are creating networks as they walk down the street – in touch with one person, then another and then the next. In the UK 11.6 *billion* text messages were sent in 2002 on O_2 phones alone.[41] Nearly half of all 25- to 34 year-olds claim that they "could not live without" their mobile phone.[42]

Individuals are not confined to communities in which they were born, nor are they just selecting from networks that already exist: they are also creating their own networks – networks that fit each person exactly. Fluid, self-constructed communities, built as you walk, are becoming part of everyday life.

These developments are creating the demand for liquid church, which will exist as much in the networks between individuals as in the gatherings of people. Instead of meeting at a fixed time in a fixed place, church will be more fluid.

A youth worker, for example, pastors up to 25 young people at the end of a mobile phone, meeting face-to-face with them in twos and threes from time to time. Three teenagers became Christians, did not integrate into their local church, but sent prayers by text "to" each other, beginning to express congregational life in miniature. The Church of England's Oxford Diocese has advertised for a "web pastor" to oversee an internet church, rooted in the traditions of one of the diocese's religious communities.[43]

Workplace church

Will new forms of church also emerge in the workplace? The interest is considerable. I am intrigued by how many people have asked me about it. In recent years, St John's has had several trainee ministers who feel called to plant church in the workplace. The strong role that jobs still play in people's lives and the continuing disconnect between Sunday and Monday is bringing workplace church on to the screen.

The 2002 Scottish Church Census found that in 2002, 120,000 fewer people were in Sunday church compared to 1994. Two-thirds of the drop were women. Half of them were aged 20 to 44. Focus groups revealed that the main reason these women were leaving was related to employment. More were working full-time, leaving less time for church, and more were in jobs requiring Sunday work.[44]

As life becomes more fluid, people are likely to adopt more flexible ideas about church. Instead of thinking "My church is St Andrew's on Sunday", a growing number may say "I belong to two churches – St Andrew's at the weekend, and my workplace church during the week". They could replace all their midweek activities at "St Andrews" with church at work. If this were to be a call from God, would weekend churches be willing to adapt?

Nods toward workplace church include Christian doctors in a health centre who hold regular healing services after hours. A former community nurse has a vision for doing something similar after she is ordained. Should she work as a community nurse with one or two other Christians, inviting patients (where appropriate) to an accessible, weekly service of healing and using this to launch a new expression of church?

A businessman asks whether he is called to become a "post-industrial" chaplain, walking with people into faith by fostering on-line networks in the workplace, which then become a form of church. A minister looks around his patch, sees workers pouring into the pubs and cafés at lunchtime and asks if he can start a workplace congregation in a restaurant. St Thomas Crookes, Sheffield, starts a cluster of 30 to 80 people with a workplace focus.

Might this last example suggest possibilities for large city-centre churches? Quite a few have a good number of home groups. Might some of these groups have a work focus, perhaps clustered together and operating on cell-church principles? Could they look for ways of serving the workplace – organising a stress clinic for example – as the first step toward a different way of being church?

Hybrids

Traditional, rooted, brand, liquid and workplace churches may of course combine with each other. A brand church might have a local or liquid dimension, for example. Indeed, all five expressions could come together in a "multiplex church".

A church u-turn?

The church is on a knife-edge. Its pulse is growing fainter as numbers drop. The challenge of inner cities and outer estates remains acute. "The big C", consumerism, has turned up the heat on Christianity. Churchgoers need to understand the seriousness of church decline and the reasons for it. They cannot go on putting the body of Christ into a hospice, to be lovingly nursed before it dies.

Yet despite its challenges, the consumer world is also creating mission opportunities. Christians need the vision to spot them – and the energy to respond. Will the church bunk off, exhausted by internal wrangles? Will it change only in ways to keep existing members happy? Or will it reach out to an exciting, if bewildering world?

Alongside some traditional ones rooted, brand, liquid and workplace churches could well flourish in the years ahead. Yet it is not clear what these new strands of church will look like – what specific forms will work in particular contexts. Hence the need to experiment, to try one thing and then another, and to learn from experience.

We do not need more churches of the kind that are struggling, but experiments that can open up new vistas – that will be messages from the future more than straws in the wind. As George Lings and Stuart Murray Williams put it, experiments are "a workshop of the Spirit".[45]

George Lings writes:

*I wonder whether Mike should have included in this chapter
a paragraph arguing – theologically – that God engages
with the world as it is, not as he wished it might be. So if
the world changes, the church should respond, to follow
God's example of engaging with reality demonstrated in the
birth and life of Christ.*

Notes

1. Graham Cray, *Youth Congregations and the Emerging Church*, Cambridge: Grove Books, 2002, p. 18.
2. George Lings, "Unit 8. Out of sight, out of nothing", *Encounters on the Edge*, No. 2, The Sheffield Centre, 1999, p. 5.
3. Peter Brierley (ed.), *UK Christian Handbook. Religious Trends 4 2003/4*, London: Christian Research, 2003, Table 2.24.1. The Church of England changed how it collected its attendance figures, which makes it difficult to compare recent trends for the UK as a whole with those before 1998. However, between 2000 and 2002 the number of people attending the Church of England at least once a week dropped by 8%, suggesting that in this denomination at least the decline is continuing.
4. *Mission-shaped Church*, London: Church House Publishing, 2004, pp. 40–41. The figures for 1980 to 2000 are based on children's attendance at Sunday worship, not Sunday school. So the total number of children connected to church through all its Sunday and midweek activities is probably significantly larger. Even so, the total will be only a small proportion of the overall child population. If the figure remained constant at the 14% in 1970 – most implausible given the numbers in Table 3.3 – 86% of young people would not be involved in any way with Sunday church.
5. Robin Gill, *Churchgoing and Christian Ethics*, Cambridge: Cambridge University Press, 1999, Chapter Seven.

6. Callum G. Brown, *The Death of Christian Britain*, London: Routledge, 2001, p. 198.

7. Steve Bruce, *God is Dead. Secularization in the West*, Oxford: Blackwell, 2002.

8. For example, an outstanding discussion of the new urban context is Laurie Green, *Urban Ministry and the Kingdom of God*, London: SPCK, 2003.

9. www.emergingchurch.info/stories/paulthomson/index.htm.

10. Brown, op. cit., especially Chapters Eight & Nine. Brown's thesis, given a twist here, has been criticised, for example by Grace Davie, *Europe: The Exceptional Case*, London: DLT, pp. 20–21.

11. Bruce, op. cit., especially Chapter 12.

12. Shoshana Zuboff and James Maxmin, *The Support Economy: Why Corporations are Failing Individuals and the Next Episode of Capitalism*, London: Allen Lane, 2002, p. 7.

13. *Measuring Child Poverty*, London: Department of Work and Pensions, 2003.

14. Commenting on the Government's proposed new measures of poverty, expert in the field Jonathan Bradshaw said, "Poverty is not about survival any more, it's about the ability to participate in the society in which we now live." *The Times*, 19 December 2003.

15. Roger Bootle, *Money for Nothing*, London: Nicholas Brealey, 2003, p. 254. Obviously, this is a huge assumption. An environmental catastophe or a prolonged major war could blow it apart. On the other hand, many experts would say it is a bit cautious.

16. London, of course, will still be out in front, and may be even further ahead. Higher living standards overall don't necessarily mean the narrowing of income inequalities.

17. This section draws heavily on Michael Moynagh, *Changing World, Changing Church*, London: Monarch, 2001, Chapter 1. As C. P. Snow once remarked, "If an author cannot quote himself, who can he quote?"

18. B. Joseph Pine II and James H. Gilmour, *The Experience*

Economy, Boston: Harvard, 1999.

19. *Essence* was developed by the Methodist evangelist, Rob Frost and is published by Kingsway and CPAS. It is available from most Christian bookshops.

20. For example, many of today's poor are pensioners. Over the next 20 years, a much higher proportion of women will retire with their own pension (because of the influx of women into the workforce over the past 40 years). This will raise pensioner household incomes significantly. At the same time many people now in their fifties and sixties will retire with relatively generous final salary occupational pensions. Younger age groups will boost their "retirement" incomes by working till they are older. See Michael Moynagh and Richard Worsley, *Opportunity of a Lifetime: The Future of Retirement*, London: CIPD, 2004, Chapters Two & Three.

21. Michael Willmott, *Citizen Brands. Putting society at the heart of your business*, Chichester: Wiley, 2001, pp. 159–62.

22. Charles Desforges, *The Impact of Parental Involvement, Parental Support and Family Education on Pupil Achievement and Adjustment: A Literature Review*, London: DfES, 2003, para. 9.4.

23. Robert D. Putnam, *Bowling Alone*, New York: Simon & Schuster, 2000.

24. *Social Trends*, London: Office of National Statistics, 2003, pp. 177–78.

25. Jonathan Gershuny & Kimberly Fisher, "Leisure" in A. H. Halsey with Josephine Webb (eds), *Twentieth Century British Social Trends*, London: Macmillan, 2000, p. 647.

26. Daniel Miller, *A Theory of Shopping*, Polity Press, 1998, esp. Chapter One.

27. Martin Robinson & Dwight Smith, *Invading Secular Space*, London: Monarch, 2003, p. 36.

28. Margaret Mark & Carol S. Pearson, *The Hero and the Outlaw*, New York: McGraw-Hill, 2001, p. 359, cited by Robinson and Smith, op. cit., p. 211.

29. American psychologist, Barry Schwartz, has been reported

as suggesting that "maximisers" who explore every option may end up with better results than "satisficers", who stop searching as soon as they have found something that suits their purpose, but they are less satisfied with what they get. Happiness may be about foregoing choice. *The Times*, 21 February 2004.

30. For example, Andrew Davey, *Urban Christianity and GlobalOrder*, London: SPCK, 2001, pp. 24–26.
31. "Changing values (2): Work and Leisure", 2 July 2003, www.mori.com/digest/2003.
32. Edmund King & David Leibling, "Commuting and travel choices",www.racfoundation.org/our_research/Commutepaper.
33. Alison Park & Ceridwen Roberts, "The ties that bind" in Alison Park et al. (eds), *British Social Attitudes: the 19th Report*, London: Sage, 2002, pp. 185–211.
34. Office of National Statistics, *Social Trends*, op. cit., p. 208.
35. Michael Moynagh & Richard Worsley, "The State of the Countryside 2020. A report to the Countryside Agency", www.countryside.gov.uk, p. 26.
36. www.emergingchurch.info/café/stories/grahamold. Reports since suggest that things may not have gone entirely as planned.
37. Rolf Jensen, *The Dream Society*, New York: McGraw-Hill, 1999, pp. 51–113.
38. Pete Ward, *Liquid Church*, Carlisle: Paternoster, 2002.
39. For example, in a speech to the Fabian Society on 17 June 2003 Tony Blair declared, "Our aim is to open up the system – to end the one-size-fits-all model of public service . . . The public, like us, want education and health services free at the point of use – but they don't want services uniform and undifferentiated at the point of use, unable to respond to their individual needs and aspirations."
40. I have discussed this more fully in Michael Moynagh, *Changing World, Changing Church*, London: Monarch, 2001, Chapter Two.

41. *What mobile can do*, mm02 corporate responsibility report 2003.
42. Research conducted by Henley Management College/Teleconomy, 2003. For details contact tim@cm-pr.co.uk.
43. For more about the internet church, see www.i-church.org.
44. Christian Research, *Quadrant*, July 2003.
45. George Lings and Stuart Murray, *Church Planting: Past, Present and Future*, Cambridge: Grove Books, 2003, p. 25.

CHAPTER FOUR

TALKING STRATEGIC SENSE

In their book on reinventing leadership for a reinvented church, Martin Robinson and Dwight Smith describe what emerging church looked like 200 years ago.

For half a century, the Wesleys and others had been experimenting with fresh expressions of church (though they would not have called it that). They had started cells to nurture people brought into faith through the great eighteenth-century revivals. They had begun to transform worship by introducing new hymns and preaching outside church buildings. They had launched a new movement which, against their intentions, became a denomination.

Yet observers of the British church in 1800 were gloomy. Dusk appeared to have fallen on the church. It did not look as if a significant spiritual movement was under way. The Christian impact on society seemed limited. It took another 50 years for the sun to shine again. Yet the seeds of Victorian Britain's evangelical revival were present, almost unnoticed, in the eighteenth-century's emerging church.[1]

Might we face a similar situation today? The inherited church is weak and losing ground. New expressions of church are spasmodic: not a few have snuffed it. Yet many Christians have been praying for a stronger church. Might emerging church be the answer to their prayers?

RISKY WORSHIP no. 43
THE KEY CHANGE

Defusing a time bomb

As emerging church spreads, the most difficult challenge for the existing church will be to back it with manpower and money. A ferment is bubbling away. The idea of emerging church is gaining ground, but the battle for resources has scarcely begun.

Emerging church should be a priority because it makes strategic sense. Every organisation is having to adapt to the new century – and the church must change too. We know that emerging church can work. Existing congregations don't have to turn themselves inside out. It is easy to start – well, quite! More resources may be available than we think. We can develop the expertise. But emerging church is not "a piece of cake" so we need to be ready to take the risks. Our starting point in this chapter is the need for radical change.

Caution reigns

The stay-as-we-are brigade are sceptical about whether emerging church can stem the haemorrhage of worshipping Christians. Why not focus on improving the existing church instead?

Statistician, researcher and minister, Bob Jackson, has put the Anglican Church through a statistical scanner and offered a diagnosis: inherited churches can indeed grow by adopting process forms of evangelism and other best practice.

In the north of England a group of large Anglican churches met over several years, comparing notes and agreeing steps that would reverse their numerical slide. Participants collectively halted their decline and even began to grow: comparable churches that didn't take part continued their downward drift.[2] "That just shows we don't need fresh expressions of church," some leaders have concluded.

Other church leaders embrace the idea of emerging church, but remain cautious. Expecting churchgoers to shunt resources from the status quo to the new frontline feels too much. Reinventing church is in the script, but the mood is still, "Let's keep an eye on these new developments, encourage them, dip our toes in the water perhaps, but not take the plunge – at least yet".

Cut and cut again?

What's needed is the exact opposite approach – keep an eye on the existing church, cherish it and encourage best practice, but make experimental church a growing priority. Why? Because time is running out.

The inherited church is drifting away from society. The number of adults with a Christian background is shrinking. Public indifference to Christianity has the church by the throat. Channelling resources into the existing church will merely prop up congregations that appeal to a smaller and smaller segment of the population.

"Doing inherited church better" might give the church a temporary reprieve, but it would not be a lasting solution. This generation would still pass on a church that was totally ill-equipped to flourish in the next. If we wait before confronting our mission context, we risk having smaller and longer-in-the-tooth congregations, with fewer and less energetic members to spark something new.

Church leaders might ask themselves, "Will we be remembered for bequeathing a church that is dying on its feet, or for laying the foundations of church with a future?"

George Lings writes:
Once again, Mike is not afraid to be clear thinking. In the older denominations, so much human and financial resource is directed to support existing expressions of church. That does not make sense when these expressions connect only with a minority percentage of the population, which is diminishing. A shift to invest in the emerging is called for.

Critics claim that emerging church is fragile – but so is the existing church![3] Many denominations are slicing back their paid staff. Despondency is widespread. It is hard to see how "doing inherited church better" can work when resources are being hacked back. People look ahead to a future something like this:

- Declining church attendance leads to reductions in paid staff.
- Fewer paid ministers mean that churches are overseen in larger groups.
- Larger groups of churches mean that more individual churches are led by lay people alone or by part-time and spare-time clergy.
- Full-time paid clergy increasingly provide specialist support to these lay leaders and part-time ministers.
- The strategy is maintenance driven – how can we keep going?
- It is almost certainly doomed. "If the church didn't grow in the past," many wonder, "why should it grow in the future, doing what it does now, but with fewer resources?"
- So today's cutbacks are likely to be a staging post – to the next round of cuts.

Can churches that are slimming down put resources into fresh church at the same time? It is a tall order. Yet as Albert Einstein once said, "It is impossible to get out of a problem by using the same kind of thinking that got you into the problem."

A changing world

The church is not the only organisation having to adapt. Organisations throughout the advanced world are reinventing themselves as torrents of change sweep down the "Oh Oh" decade. At the cutting edge are three themes.

- *Experimentation.* Old ways do not work any more. But what will work is far from clear. Even if we knew what to do, change is so rapid, procedures are so quickly out of date and human interactions are now so numerous at work

("Can I speak to so-and-so?" "Sorry, they're in a meeting") that one set of rules will not cover all circumstances.[4] Teams keep breaking the boundaries. So in progressive organisations devolving responsibility, allowing units to experiment, tolerating failure and learning from success is becoming the order of the day.

- *Personalisation.* Describing the modern corporation, Shoshana Zuboff and James Maxmin observe, "People have changed more than the business organisations on which they depend. . . . The chasm that now separates individuals and organisations is marked by frustration, mistrust, disappointment and even rage."[5]

  Tom Bentley and James Wilsdon of the London-based think-tank, Demos, have written about the public services, "We still rely on a shared social context that is bigger than ourselves, but we are less ready to submit to standardised relationships with large, impersonal organisations . . . To use resources effectively, services must be personalised."[6]

- *New forms of scale.* Personalisation requires new configurations of scale. In the standardised world, increasing a factory's output reduced the costs of each unit. These economies of scale are no longer enough. Personalisation demands new types of scale, as organisations pool their resources – cooperation by specialist secondary schools, for example. Current thinking is that eventually each school in a town will have a different specialism, so that pupils and staff can take advantage of the maths expertise in one school for instance, and the sports expertise in another. Individuals will have more scope to develop their gifts.

Emerging church raises similar issues. How can the church promote experiments? How can it be "personalised" to different cultural groups? How can churches cooperate to produce new forms of scale that support a contextualised approach?

Fresh expressions of church make sense because they reflect a "social quake" that is forcing organisations into new shapes.

Like the rest of the world, the church cannot stand still – and survive.

A dud prospectus? Not at all!

"Show me examples that have been going for a long time", the leader of one mega church said to me, "and I'll give it a go." A second reason for bringing emerging church on to centre stage is that it is not built on quicksand: these examples do exist.

Evidence! Evidence!

Bob Jackson analysed a database of 369 Anglican church plants over a 23-year period, held by the Church Army's Sheffield Centre. An average of about 27 people helped launch these plants. Three or four years later, average attendance was around 70 – a sensational increase of 250%.

Did these plants grow through transfer from other, less exciting congregations? Jackson cites a mid-1990s survey of 90 (different) church plants. Twenty per cent of attenders were the original planting team, a further 16% had transferred from other churches, but the remaining 64% were mainly not transfers. "Well over half were new to churchgoing."[7]

By no means all the plants in the Sheffield database were fresh expressions of church: many would have been replicas of the existing church. Not all the plants may have survived longer term. Some early failures may be excluded from the figures. Even so, it is clear that despite disappointments church planting can lead to growth. This is especially true when it is tailored to specific cultural groups.[8]

Jackson argues strongly for such an approach. Addressing the Church of England, he claims "the Church must perforce be multicultural in its own expression. Ideally, a parish church should aim to offer worship and church life in and to all the main subcultures of its parish – a traditional service, a youth service, a child-friendly service, a jazz service, and so on."[9]

The principle is clear: the more options available, the more routes people will find into the church. Widening choice expands access.

Examples are multiplying of emerging churches that do work.

Around 16 churches from different denominations in Folkestone, Kent are collaborating to create new expressions of church for young people. Under the banner "What 4", they have clubbed together to appoint eleven town-wide youth workers, with funding from central and local government, charitable trusts and the churches themselves.

These youth workers are spearheading a variety of before-school, after-school and lunchtime clubs for children and teenagers. Christian young people meet at school in groups of twelve to 35 for prayer, worship, spiritual instruction and planning. Some help to lead lunchtime and other clubs for non-believers, run on an "open" youth club model. Others support The Base and The Zone, weekly clubs at either end of the town where young people can learn to skateboard and take part in other activities. Others are involved in the very popular "canoe school".

Through friendships formed in these different settings, non-churchgoing young people are invited to one-off Christian events or to an *Alpha* group, which is tailored to the particular youngsters on the course. Young people who start entering the Christian faith may be drawn into one of the schools-based Christian groups or to one of the teenage congregations in the town.

If they stay with the faith, they will be encouraged to support other emerging Christians on their journeys. Eventually, they may become a "schools worker" – mainly older teenagers still at school, who receive special training in how to advance the Kingdom in the classroom and among their peers.

"Hope for the Church" certainly includes fresh expressions of church. As in Folkestone, many are developing a track record to envy. But are there enough examples?

Steadily more bold

The danger is that church leaders set the bar too high. They demand more evidence than is available, and in its absence they refuse to back emerging church. Lacking support, experiments dribble out at a turtle's pace. Doubts about the evidence hold back initiatives that could have produced the evidence. Meanwhile, churchgoers get older by the day, till by the time they are persuaded to act they lack the energy and resources to do so.

Yet can we avoid being foolhardy? A "sensible shoes" approach might roll out experiments gradually as resources become available, with feedback to the wider church. Each step might be slightly ahead of the evidence, but not so far in front as to be too risky.

This would move the existing church into the unknown and widen the horizon for learning. Inherited church could pull back, change direction or move ahead more rapidly in the light of the results. Emerging church would earn it spurs and make the case for further resources.

The more time and money spent now on building an evidence-base, the quicker the church will learn – and the faster it will adapt to a cyber-paced world.

We don't have to turn ourselves inside out

A third strategic argument for emerging church is that you don't have to transform the existing church to start something different.

There are exceptions, of course. Some new forms of church do turn the existing church inside out. If it is done properly, for instance, cell church may involve the whole congregation in a new way of being church – more outward looking and with a much stronger focus on the small group. But many churchgoers are not for turning.

Something new with something old

God was clearly present in the worship of one congregation. Visiting preachers used to comment on it. Yet humanly speaking, if you looked at the congregation's age structure and the difficulty it had in attracting new people, you would have to conclude that its lifespan was about 30 years. By then, on current trends, it will be a rump.

So what might one do? A minister might battle away to "modernise" the service and make it more appealing to outsiders. But opposition would mount, people would be upset, energy would be squandered in conflict and the changes required might be so large that the congregation would end up with a completely alien style of worship. Members might be so miserable that no outsider would want to join!

Of course it wouldn't come to that. There would be compromises. Some small changes would be introduced – perhaps a few more modern songs. But how many people flock to church because the congregation is singing a couple more contemporary songs? Tiptoeing steps by the existing church will get nowhere near the surrounding culture.

So why bother? The assumption that there is something wrong with the existing church – that the church must change to reach outsiders – is pastorally damaging. It immediately puts the congregation on the back foot ("there's nothing wrong with us!"). It is also inconsistent. If cultural diversity is legitimate outside church, it should be encouraged inside church. What is wrong with an inherited style of worship that brings people close to God?

Might it not be better to affirm the congregation in its existing culture, praise God for blessings over the years, encourage members to be open to anything new the Spirit might bring, and look for ways of planting new forms of church alongside the old? Docking a new expression of church on to the mainstream may be a more effective way of reaching non-churchgoers than revamping an existing congregation. Reproduction may be easier than resurrection.

You can have your cake and eat it

After I had suggested this to a gathering of rural church leaders, one minister wrote: ". . . your comment on not changing the

'base unit' to the point that those who belong don't recognise and appreciate themselves has encouraged a number of churches to realise that they can keep what they value, while creating the new alongside . . . There has been some very good discussion in our church councils, where many things formerly accepted were challenged."

Many in the pews recognise that the church has to move on. Yet often they resist new ideas because they would have to give up too much. Starting afresh makes change a lot easier. Churchgoers are asked to surrender less, to nourish what they have and to make it possible for others to be church "in their own voice" too. Church can suit other people just as it suits existing members.

We can get cracking

Another strategic plus is that emerging church can be easy to start. It doesn't have to be complicated. "Seeker services", for instance, may involve drama, presentation songs, audio-visual media, testimonies and "issue-based" talks, designed to encourage non-believers to explore the Christian faith further.

Some churches have found them highly effective. But they are not easy. They take time to create, arrange and rehearse. They need people with talent. They are best done regularly – once a month or so. For many churches, it is all too much. Other fresh expressions of church are simpler.

Within reach

I was speaking about emerging church to one congregation in a run-down neighbourhood. As I looked round the 30 people present, some were preoccupied with children, others seemed tired and others were distinctly old. I wondered quietly, "Is anyone going to be interested in this?"

After the service, an older woman exclaimed, "Thank you, for what you said. It's given me an idea. I live in sheltered accommodation. I'm going to invite some of my neighbours to form a sewing circle, and I am going to ask the minister to come in at the end to lead a few prayers. Who knows! This could be the start of a new congregation."

In another church was a hairdresser. Her cell group was discussing whether they could invite their non-believing friends. "I couldn't invite my friends to this group," she thought. "But I could invite some of my non-churchgoing clients to my home for prayer, especially if I did the praying."

Emerging church need not be a complex model. It's a mindset – a mindset that can free up ordinary people in the pews. Any congregation will have some members who are born networkers. One or two of them may be able to draw their friends together, and, perhaps with help, start the beginnings of a spiritual group.

Fringe benefits

Many churches have low-hanging fruit on their doorsteps. They run groups on the fringe, such as meetings for women and older people, most of whom may not attend on Sunday. Two studies – in London, and in Yorkshire and Humberside – found that at 13,500 the number of church community projects, including children and youth activities, almost doubled the number of churches![10]

It is often a struggle to build bridges from these groups into main church. Individuals are comfortable in their groups, but for hosts of reasons find the existing church unattractive. Church can seem so culturally alien! Emerging church says "You don't need to battle with these bridges any more. It may be possible for church to spring up within these groups."

If the members agreed, for example, a luncheon club might have a period of quiet prayer at the end of its meeting. Part of the room might be set aside for the purpose, with candles and some quiet Christian music. Individuals could stay behind if they wished. Chapter Two has a rural example.

Other churches have built up relationships within a group, invited individuals to a separate discussion and then allowed this new "cell" to evolve into its own expression of church. The next chapter describes an urban drop-in centre that gave birth to a new congregation.

A discussion group, for example, might start with an exploration of spirituality (possibly using the *Essence* material), then it might plunder the *Y-course* (for people who are nowhere near ready for *Alpha*), then it might use the CPAS *Start* course (repeating material as necessary) and then perhaps use *Emmaus*, which has an emphasis on discipleship. By the end, the group would be learning, praying and worshipping together – the beginnings of a congregation.

> ### George Lings writes:
> *These are good illustrations of what I think is a principle. You could call it "ecclesia seeks agora" – that means, to non-Greek speakers, that church is something that finds where people gather and then begins to grow itself within or on to that natural expression of community. Church is not imported complete, but grows organically as people from that gathering are encountered by Jesus and changed.*

New ways of being church offer a chance to cross the unintentional ravine between community and spiritual development. They can do this by abandoning the "you come to us" model – "Let's hope that people in the community project find their way into church on Sunday." Instead, they look for ways of spiritually nurturing the group, with the support of those involved. Fresh expressions can add spiritual value to community engagement.

Emerging church may also be an answer to groups which have done *Alpha*, but find that participants are reluctant to move on to church. *Alpha* graduates peep round the door of mainstream church and reel, "I could never cope with that!" Jane Gibbs, a minister's wife, has written about the suburban church:

Each time an Alpha course runs in our suburban parish, a handful of new Christians emerge. But these same *Alpha* graduates (unlike those in our inner city experience) rarely become regular church attenders. "The group wants to stay together", we have agreed, so over the years we have devised more and more programmes (Beta, Gamma . . .) for the group to do midweek. So we create yet another separate congregation.'[11]

Her worry is that these new "congregations" fail to integrate with the rest of church.

Look inside

Some congregations may not need to look outside their doors, even, to launch a new expression of church. Perhaps they have a small group of twenties and thirties – or older – who are hanging on to church by their finger nails.

The group could be invited to explore other ways of being church, ways that might also appeal to their friends. Rather than peeling away from church and adding to the statistics of decline, individuals might be re-energised and invite friends to something different. The church would grow instead.

Why travel from A to Z to try emerging church, when A to B will do?

We have the resources

A fifth reason for trialling new forms of church is that, by and large, the resources exist. That is not the perception of most people, of course. Even church leaders enthused by emerging church often shrink from pouring time and money into it – a crunch test of people's seriousness.

"Our minister won't be replaced" is not an uncommon lament. Or the lucky large churches think, "We've got so much going on, we can't afford any more commitments." Many churchgoers are no longer mesmerised by the status quo. They warm to the idea of emerging church, but are reluctant to pay for it. So they prevaricate. They react like the American baseball player, Yogi Berra, "I came to a fork in the road, and took it."

A privileged church

Do we have the people and money for emerging church? Compared to parts of Africa and Asia, many denominations and streams in the advanced world church are awash with resources. The Church of England may be struggling, for example, but it has over 12,500 licensed clergy, of whom nearly 9,500 are paid.[12] It has more youth workers than assistant clergy (curates) and tens of thousands of volunteers. Churches in poorer parts of the world would be thrilled with just a fraction of these paid and unpaid workers.

One bishop met with representatives from some Church of England rural parishes. Forty-two clergy and readers were present. Only six received a stipend. But when they added up the time that was given by part-timers and spare-timers, they had the equivalent of 13 full-time members of staff. In terms of licensed ministry, these churches were probably as well off as they were 20 years ago. They had more professionals than they realised.

The problem is not inadequate resources, but how they are used. In many denominations and "streams", the existing church consumes so much time and energy that little is left for the wider community. As denominations retrench, maintaining the inherited church becomes even harder. Can resources be shifted to new forms of mission at the same time?

In particular, what about churches with a strong eucharistic tradition? Wouldn't new expressions of church crush their over-worked priests, especially where one priest is "looking after" several churches?

Maybe the answer will lie in encouraging locally ordained ministers. Or perhaps innovative ways of celebrating Holy Communion can be found, without taxing priests still further – extended Communions and agape suppers possibly, or bringing congregations together for a social event with Communion at its heart. Expectations would have to change of course, but what are the alternatives?

Large churches shouldn't purr

Big churches are vital. Many have large staff and are financially well off compared to smaller churches. A number look healthy enough, but a peek below the floorboards can reveal shaky foundations.

Between 1989 and 1998, only 10% of Church of England churches with over 400 adults on a Sunday actually grew; more than 70% declined. Large churches performed worse than for every category of smaller church. A tiny number of extra large churches seemed to be doing slightly better, but – as a group – not much more than holding their own.[13]

Anecdotal evidence suggests that when large churches do grow, frequently it is because they are recycling the saints. Christian students and young professionals move to a new area, for example, and gravitate to a well-known (large) church. Individuals may swap their smaller church for a larger one with better children's and other programmes – what retailers call "cannibalising the market": one church eats up members from another.

Large churches with "successful" outreach programmes often attract mainly lapsed Christians. The Berlin Wall between church and people with no church experience has yet to be breached. The leaders of one large town centre church, which was growing phenomenally, asked how many members had come to faith from no Christian background. They knew of just seven.

Yet the number of people with some church background is plummeting. Fewer and fewer fish remain in the river: the real catch is out at sea. Large churches might ask themselves how effectively they are using their resources to reach people who have had no contact with church. How many new members in this category can they actually count?

There is evidence of a "glass ceiling" beyond which churches struggle to grow (unless they have more paid staff). This ceiling is probably in the area of 100 to 150 adults. If it is punctured, churches may encounter further ceilings higher up.[14] One way to smash through these ceilings is to break the church into smaller units. People then feel more involved and committed.

Planting new forms of church, tailored to specific cultural groups, is an obvious way to do that. Someone who feels on the edge of a large congregation, which is not their style anyway, will be more likely to attend a smaller group where they feel at home.

Some jumbo churches run huge *Christianity Explored*, *Alpha* or other such courses to explore the Christian faith. Why not turn each course into a new congregation? If a large church ran one course every twelve months and encouraged it to go on meeting at the same time in the same style, it could plant a new congregation each year! As new members learnt to give, they would soon afford a part-time pastor.

Large churches are crucial because of their size and resources. The sheer number of Christians involved means that if you turn them around, you will turn the church as a whole round. But many are complacent. Their size and busy-ness masks their failure to reach perhaps the fastest growing "people group" in the advanced world – individuals with no church experience.

Geologists know that the lack of rumbling can be deceptive. An earthquake can still take place, even though no one noticed. That doesn't make it harmless. A silent quake can presage a devastating shock later. Might this be the fate of large churches? The ground is moving today, but to many it is silent. If these churches refuse to embrace new forms of mission, will their foundations be shaken apart tomorrow?

Releasing lay people

A key challenge for both large and small churches is to release lay people. Many churchgoers are well placed to help start fresh expressions of church.

One denominational leader met with 25, rather discouraged churchgoers. He asked them what clubs and organisations they belonged to, and what offices they held. They were amazed to discover how influential they were, as a group, in their local community. Could they use their networks to advance the church's mission?

Christians on a large housing estate in the east of England did exactly that. The estate had an unusually high number of older people. Over seven years, a variety of activities sprang up to meet their needs, from a luncheon club to regular outings. On an individual basis, Christians from various churches had thrown themselves into the different organisations.

One person had the bright idea of bringing these Christians together. Between them they knew 300 or so older people. "Why don't we do something specifically Christian with those who want it?" So they organised a Sunday afternoon tea with high quality food at a modest price. They included a testimony, a short prayer and some Christian music, the beginnings of a Christian congregation.

Fifty people came. They were so enthused that they invited their friends. "But I don't go to church" one person said. "It's not like church" came the reply. The leaders have now run an *Alpha* course, which has led to a fortnightly cell.

Stuart Murray Williams writes:
This story, like several others in the book, is really an example of a mission initiative that may in time develop into a new congregation. Is it helpful to label this "emerging church"? Maybe – as long as the emphasis is on "emerging" rather than "church". Time alone will tell how many of Mike's stories result in viable churches.

Sometimes lay people only need the idea and their leaders' support, and they will launch a new expression of church. Others may be enthusiastic, but need releasing from commitments to the existing church.

Might churches take a risk? Leaders could say, "Let's invite members of the congregation to get involved with a fresh expression of church. If that means giving up a task within the church, let's encourage them to do so and pray that someone else will fill the hole. After all, if they moved away we would have to find a replacement. So why don't we treat volunteers for emerging church as if they had moved? Surely we can trust God to help fill the gaps."

Put it in the job description!

Imagine that every minister, every assistant minister, every youth worker and every evangelist had "Spend two days a week on emerging church" in their job descriptions (or as an explicit expectation). Fresh expressions of church would surge dramatically! Of course, many people would object. Could the inherited church cope if paid staff gave significant time to emerging church?

One businessman described how his company expects to use 60% of staff time serving existing customers and 40% chasing new ones. "If someone is ill, we all manage. But if I suggest redeploying a person to these new customers, everyone complains: 'We can't survive without her'. So I reply, 'Here's someone who has been off work for several months. You coped without her. Why don't you go on surviving, while I redeploy her to a different job?'"

Might the church adopt a similar approach? Often there is a time lag between when the minister (or another member of staff) leaves and their successor arrives – as much as a year or 18 months. During that time the church survives, and even flourishes.

Suppose that the new person was asked to spend three days on continuing church and two on new forms of church. The existing church would have three more days of the person's time than when they had no one at all. Not a bad deal!

It would raise all sorts of concerns, obviously. "If the new person spends only three days a week on the existing church, who's going to do all the other jobs their predecessor did?" Whoever was doing them in the interregnum might be an answer. Committees made excellent decisions about new paving stones, when the church should be locked up and arrangements for the next social with no minister present. Why can't they go on meeting without the minister, except when a clergy presence is vital?

Or maybe the new person settles into their job, does not have time to do the rotas (which their predecessor had done) and asks for a volunteer. Betty steps forward. She would have done it five years ago, but no one asked.

Perhaps someone doesn't offer. That could be a sign that the task is not so vital after all – at least, not as important as reaching out through new forms of church. Or maybe someone else can fill the gap, but only if their "job" is allowed to lapse. Might pruning the vine to bear fruit be an appropriate image (John 15:1–2)?

Step by step

Possibly paid and other staff could be released on a gradual basis. A church might decide that when their youth worker leaves, the next one will have emerging church high on the agenda. Possibly the existing youth worker could be invited to prepare the ground.

Maybe a new assistant minister could be tasked with developing a fresh form of Christian community. In the Church of England, for instance, a diocese might decide that one of its full-time curates (trainee ministers) will be put into a situation with opportunities for a fresh expression of church. The curate might be expected to spend half their time on continuing and half on emerging church.

Arguably, this is exactly the sort of training that ministers need for tomorrow's church. If they are not given the opportunity to experiment with church when their training minister is at hand to support, advise and encourage them, what is the chance of them pioneering when they carry the whole can themselves?[15]

Derek Spencer is a curate in the Church of England. He was appointed a Deanery Youth Missioner in Storrington Deanery, West Sussex by the Bishop of Horsham, who had a vision for a youth congregation there. After two years of preparation, thought and prayer, Derek picked a leadership team of seven from churches in the area to help lead the new venture, which they named "Eden" – starting from the beginning. One hundred and twenty to 150 young people have attended their initial monthly services in a local grammar school.

Having been in post for two years, Derek was ordained in December 2003 and is now serving his curacy in this job context. ". . . it's a positive sign of the Church of England taking a risk, breaking out of the mould and being a bit more flexible and imaginative. It also gives me the authority to carry this vision forward and in time, hopefully, establish this Church within the area and incorporate the whole life of the church within it."[16]

Many clergy will feel that they were called into a more conventional ministry, and that they are not equipped to launch new expressions of church. But could they encourage other people to do so and provide appropriate support? Might they even encourage their lay people to consider whether the next minister should be asked to make emerging church a priority? Preparing the ground could be the best contribution to multitrack church many clergy can make.

When I suggested this recently, with some trepidation, to a gathering of rural church leaders, the response came as a surprise. "Could my church council discuss it now?" the chairperson asked.

Too many cradles and not enough graves?

Sociologist Robin Gill has convincingly argued that for over a century Britain has been over-churched. Keeping all the buildings open has sapped precious resources.[17] Won't planting more congregations just add to today's surfeit of churches in parts of the West?

The problem is not that we have too many congregations: we have too many congregations that are failing to reproduce. Indeed, the disease Gill diagnosed was too many *buildings* rather than too many congregations. Some fresh expressions of

church could ease this. They could be planted into existing church buildings, increasing the number of people who use the buildings and pay for their upkeep.

> One United Reformed Church District closed an inner-city congregation that was in decline and dispirited. A few moments later they reopened it with a new leadership and new vision for what church could be in that area. The new congregation began to thrive and grow.[18]

> Moot began in January 2003 as 15 people from all over London. They had been involved in alternative worship and other forms of experimental church. They started with a large sheet of paper and a projector. Since then, they have developed into an "emerging church spiritual community", with Sunday evening alternative worship services and discussions during the week. By the end of the year they had swelled to 30. Two artists in residence had joined them, and the Bishop of London had offered to license an unpaid curate (who would seek to raise his own salary) to help them develop as an emerging church. They meet in an old church building called St Matthew's, Westminster.[19]

We shall reap what we sow

Over the years many churches have used their resources selfishly. Lay volunteers have concentrated on activities for church members. Ministers have been expected to spend most of their time with their congregations. When lay staff have been appointed, often they have been expected to support work among existing churchgoers – a musical director possibly, or a youth worker for the teenage children of church members. People outside the church have been relatively unaffected.

Are we now reaping what we have sown? We have sowed the selfish use of our resources by putting them mainly into maintenance. Is it a coincidence that we are now reaping church decline? If we gave more of our resources away – by devoting them to people who don't come to church, serving them and supporting them in their spiritual quests – might we stand a chance of reaping church growth?

> ***Stuart Murray Williams writes:***
> *Excessive time spent by staff and volunteers running their church rather than engaging in mission beyond their church is rightly regarded as selfish (as well as being institutionally suicidal in a post-Christendom context). We should stop complaining that 80% of the work needed to run a church is done by 20% of the people: 20% of the people should be ample, releasing the rest to get on with mission. But will emerging churches fare any better?*

We can get the expertise

Do we have the resources? Yes, but we don't use them properly. Do we have the expertise, however? That is very different.

What skills do we need?

Any generalisation about emerging church is high-risk because fresh expressions come in many shapes, from a gathering of friends to a congregation birthed in a community project.

With that in mind, what would be the minimum skills needed to develop a new form of church in a school, or among a group of mums, or with individuals in a community centre or among some friends? The following might be a start:

- *Initiating skills.* Starting new things requires gifts of imagination, creative thinking and motivation. Pioneers see possibilities rather than problems.
- *Networking skills.* Some people have an instinctive knack of drawing individuals together. Without such a person, it may be hard to get a new group off the ground.
- *Facilitation skills.* Someone who can help the group to gel, to function properly and be a good experience for those who come will be vital to keep the group going. These community-building skills are very different to leading a

formal meeting, such as a "traditional" church service.
- *Resource skills.* Often emerging church does not need a gifted teacher or evangelist because resource material can do it for you. A gifted "you learn from me" teacher may be the last person that is needed, anyway. What's required is someone to find the suitable material, and perhaps work with the facilitator to adapt it. The amount of material, increasingly Net-based, is growing all the time.

Many congregations have individuals with one or more of these skills. Church members frequently use them in their jobs, or running a home group or out in the community. Some ministers have them, or will have the capacity to be coached in them.

Church with attitude?

These skills are not enough on their own. The bottom line is a mission mindset. Pioneers of emerging church need to understand thoroughly the principles involved, such as those in Chapter Two. Emerging church is not the same as inherited church. It does not encourage seekers to join an existing congregation, as with traditional evangelism. Nor does it expect to imprint on to a group an assumed model of church. It is experimental, flexible and responsive to culture. Pioneers need the right attitude.

Next, although some people have blazed a trail without even realising it was emerging church, others will need their imaginations stretched with concrete examples – not to copy, but to provoke ideas.

In addition, pioneers need the experience of others. Individuals who have trod a similar path may warn against pitfalls, inspire a novel approach, suggest ways of punching through a problem and – in time – generate a corpus of good practice to draw on. Innovators will need support and encouragement, as well as being held generously to account.

So although initiating, networking, facilitating and resource-gathering skills may be available, what's often lacking is knowledge – an understanding of the basic principles, a vision for what is possible and an opportunity to learn from others.

We're just beginning

This knowledge gap is beginning to be filled. To take just three examples in the UK, Sheffield-based Bob and Mary Hopkins coach catalysts of emerging church, and have started a training course to multiply the number of coaches. They are involved with ReSource, sponsored by ten Christian agencies and denominations, which has begun to offer training in church planting within the emerging culture.[20] One of those agencies is CMS, which has a Mission Movement Team that supports fresh expressions of church as part of its work. Other resources can be found through the websites in the Appendix.

As emerging church gathers pace, more initiatives will plug the knowledge deficit. The Church of England's recent report for example, *Mission-shaped Church*, has called for measures to train lay people and clergy in fresh expressions of church.[21] Making emerging church a priority should involve uncaging resources to build much-needed expertise.

Taking the risk

Emerging church is blinking on the radar, but for many it is still on the edge of the screen. The church will not offset decline by persisting with the methods that brought decline. Evidence exists that emerging church offers a more promising future. Experiments do not require the existing church to be turned inside out, they can be relatively easy to start, we have the resources (but don't use them very well) and many churchgoers have the necessary skills. There is a knowledge deficit, but initiatives are beginning to put this right – and more will follow.

However, it is still early days. Emerging church has yet to bank a bulky wadge of successes. Many experiments have failed, which makes emerging church somewhat risky. But might risk be a compelling reason for making emerging church a priority?

In today's risk-averse climate, fresh expressions of church would be distinctly counter-cultural. They would make a strong statement about the faith and hope that sustain risk.

The end of Matthew's Gospel describes how the disciples again encounter the risen Lord. They see him face to face. Yet despite all that they had seen – miraculous healings, walking on the water, turning water into wine, feeding the five thousand, raising Lazarus from the dead and now the resurrection of Jesus himself – some (the Greek could read all) still doubted.

What was Jesus' response? He entrusted to these disciples the future of the church – "Go and make disciples of all nations" (NIV). From Jesus' point of view, that must have seemed a very risky venture. How many church leaders today would entrust a critical mission to churchgoers full of doubt?

Risk was there at the beginning of the church. Ever since, at every move forward, whenever the church has made a significant advance, risk has been there again. Individuals have stepped out to the unknown, unsure what the results would be, and others have benefited.

Risk is in the very lifeblood of the church. It is integral to mission. So if making emerging church a priority feels risky, might that not be a sign that the Spirit is with us? Might it not suggest that, as in 1800, we could be on the threshold of something new?

Notes

1. Martin Robinson and Dwight Smith, *Invading Secular Space: Strategies for Tomorrow's Church*, London: Monarch, 2003, pp. 65–70.
2. Bob Jackson, *Hope for the Church*, London: Church House, 2002, pp. 43–44.
3. See for example the excellent analysis by Steven Croft, *Transforming Communities*, London: DLT, 2002, Chapter Two.
4. In a survey of a wide range of occupations up and down the

skills ladder, in nearly every case it was reported that the time spent interacting with people had increased between 1992 and 1997. Francis Green et al., "Are British workers getting more skilled?" in A. B. Atkinson & J. Hills (eds), *Exclusion, Employment and Opportunity*, London: LSE, 1998, pp. 89–131.

5. Shoshana Zuboff and James Maxmin, *The Support Economy: Why Corporations are Failing Individuals and the Next Episode of Capitalism*, London: Allen Lane, 2002, p. 4.

6. Tom Bentley and James Wilsdon, "Introduction: the adaptive state" in Tom Bentley and James Wilsdon (eds), *The Adaptive State. Strategies for personalising the public realm*, London: Demos, 2003, p. 20.

7. *Ibid.*. pp. 136–38.

8. A less rosy picture of recent church planting, stressing the pitfalls and shortcomings, is provided by George Lings and Stuart Murray, *Church Planting: Past, Present and Future*, Evangelism Series 61, Cambridge: Grove Books, 2003.

9. *Ibid.*, p. 171.

10. Christian Research, *Quadrant*, March 2003.

11. Jane Gibbs, *Faith in Suburbia*, Pastoral Series 95, Cambridge: Grove Books, 2003, p. 19.

12. Peter Brierley (ed.), *UK Christian Handbook. Religious Trends 4*, London: Christian Research, 2003, p. 8.3.

13. Bob Jackson, op. cit., pp. 108–09.

14. *Ibid.*, p. 121.

15. The Church of England report, *Mission-shaped Church* (London: Church House Publishing, 2004, p. 147), has called for curates to be placed in contexts where they can experience fresh expressions of church. This may need the rules about moving curates on after three years or so to be relaxed, so that pioneers don't leave at just the wrong time for the new expression.

16. www.emergingchurch.info/stories/eden/index.htm.

17. Robin Gill, *A Vision for Growth*, London: SPCK, 1994, Chapter Three.

18. Robinson and Smith, op. cit., p. 83.
19. www.emergingchurch.info.
20. www.resourcechurchplanting.com.
21. *Mission-shaped Church,* op. cit., p. 147.

CHAPTER 5

A U-CHURCH FOR AN I-WORLD?

New forms of church have a platinum opportunity to become more than a mere "pimple" on the surface of life. They can offload damaged baggage from the past to declare war on the dark side of consumerism. But will pioneers want to lead spiritual SAS patrols, fighting for social change? Will they be willing to shock with the new – with revolutionary forms of church that knock out the diseased cells of consumer life?

Sceptics shake their heads. "It's a sell out!" they exclaim, "consumerism wrapped in spiritual clothes." The charge is often hurled at emerging church. In reality, the boot should be on the other foot. Selling out applies at least as much to the inherited church, perhaps even more so.

> *Stuart Murray Williams writes:*
> *Criticisms of emerging churches made by members of inherited churches often seem to ignore the reality that the very things they criticise are already present (sometimes in abundance) in their own churches. Pointing a finger at others often means there are three fingers pointing back at ourselves – try it and see!*

All too often the existing church has aped the surrounding culture. It has gathered "birds of a feather", at the expense of diversity and inclusiveness. It has embraced an individualism that undermines community. It has fostered dependency – on the minister, for example. It has bred a me-based faith, which emphasises "my salvation", "my healing" or "my experience" – not an outlook to champion the less fortunate. The church has gone native.

Can emerging church do better? This is more than an item for "Question Time": it goes to the heart of how Christians experiment with fresh expressions of church.

> ### George Lings writes:
> *This chapter is very effective at helping us realise that all expressions of church are vulnerable to the charge of consumerism and that this tendency needs resisting in creating new ones. But the existing church so often fails to see that it has the same problem, perhaps even more so. Elderly, white, female and middle class are words that come to mind.*

Menu mindset

The inherited church has long mirrored the fragmentation of society. For years, middle-class people used to attend some Anglican churches in the morning and the servants went in the evening. Divisions have continued as worshippers criss-cross town to their preferred type of church.

Might emerging church be the final surrender to fragmentation? Will congregations deliberately tailored to almost every taste be more like a fixed menu with umpteen separate dishes than a smorgasbord, in which the dishes are mixed together?

This would be a travesty of the New Testament. "There is neither Jew nor Greek, slave nor free, male nor female; for you are all one in Christ Jesus" (Galatians 3:28). Do we really want a church in which children, teenagers and adults are kept apart, or where adults meet only with others like themselves?

A world of differences

Scripture affirms cultural diversity. Differences are not an end in themselves, but a basis for unity. After the Flood, for instance, God makes a covenant with Noah in which he repeats the blessings of Genesis 1:28ff. (Genesis 9:1ff.). Genesis 10 describes the outworking of this blessing. Three times it repeats the phrase, "These are the descendents of . . . in their lands, with their own language, by their families, in their nations" (verses 5, 20, 31). Different cultures are part of God's blessing.

Following the Tower of Babel debacle, these differences give rise to the scattering of the nations in Chapter Eleven. Cultural diversity becomes a punishment for the people's spiritual arrogance. The punishment does not lie in the existence of different languages, but in the people's inability to understand each other. Diversity is intrinsically good, but the division it gives rise to is not.

As we saw in Chapter Two, Pentecost sought to reverse that division by enabling the apostles to communicate in different languages – to build bridges across culture. Difference is both affirmed and jumped.

Authentic unity is not based on asking people to give up their cultures and be the same as everyone else. That is uniformity, which fails to respect people for who they are. Still worse, as we have seen, bringing everyone together in our fallen world often enables the most powerful to dominate the rest.

Unity between cultures is only authentic if I engage with you in your culture, bringing with me my culture, and we find ways of relating across our distinctive outlooks. Unity starts by respecting the worth that exists in different groups. So the church must take the fragmentation of society seriously and seek a Christian presence within each fragment – join the fragments first to join the fragments up. "Multi-cultural" church should be a melting pot.

Joined-up church

There are endless ways in which the church can draw "tribes" together – and not just in worship: for example, social events like a barn dance, a Farsee meal or a sports day; a church weekend or holiday; Christian festivals such as Spring Harvest or the Walsingham Pilgrimage; conferences, Lent groups, study evenings, day courses and retreats involving people from various churches; members of one congregation visiting those from a different culture another in their homes; inviting different gatherings to work with one other Christian group at least once a year, to serve the wider community.[1]

> Twice a year for a month one church introduced "Ten to Ten". Its 9.30 congregation had an initial act of worship, as normal. Members of the 11 o'clock congregation then joined them at ten to ten for a choice of three "sermon" activities – perhaps an interactive Bible study, a lecture-style presentation on a contemporary issue or an informal talk and discussion on a theme from "spirituality". Everyone met together for refreshments at 10.30, and then the eleven o'clock congregation had its rather different act of worship, but without the sermon.

Increasingly, "Smile please, you're on camera!" will feature in church. Video clips from one gathering will inform prayer in another. As technology upgrades at hyper speed, a town-wide youth congregation for instance will be able to screen personal stories in some of its sponsoring churches.

Meshing churches together, both inherited and emerging, will be vital in the new century. But it will require Christians with big hearts, who are willing to sink their differences for the sake of the greater whole.

More and more, individuals are best served when organisations network with each other. Church is no exception. Christians from across town or several villages can create a "critical mass" that makes possible an exhibition, a festival or work with addicts. Assembling believers together enriches each person's experience of church. Dreary church can become church with panache.

Liquid worship

Rushing toward us is "liquid worship". This is set to revolutionise our concepts of worship. It will create whole new ways of bringing diverse people together. Individuals will be able to mix-'n'-match different worship activities at the same event.[2]

> For example, at St John's College, Nottingham one service began with everyone together in the chapel. People then had 45 minutes to visit one or more "zones" scattered round the building – intercessory prayer with the aid of newspaper cuttings, prayer ministry, silent prayer with quiet music and candles, a prayer labyrinth, a video-ed sermon (repeated every 20 minutes), a discussion forum and continuing song-based worship in the chapel. Individuals could move from one zone to the next, or stay in the same zone as they wished.
>
> Some were worried we might lose the sense of community that comes from all being in the same place at once. In practice, individuals talked to each other as they walked from one zone to another, which some people thought was more community-building than staring at the back of the neck in front of you. At the end people reassembled for a brief celebration of Holy Communion, followed by supper.
>
> A year later we repeated the experiment, but in an all-age version. We had a variety of worship zones in which different ages could do activities together – from praying silently to modelling a Bible story in plasticine.

Liquid worship respects diversity: people have different ways of learning and worshipping, they come to church with different experiences in the previous week (a bereaved person may not feel able to sing "praise" songs) and they will be at different stages in their spiritual journeys. It also brings people together – perhaps around Communion before sharing refreshments.

Is this something that can be done only in a theological college with lots of rooms? A number of youth groups have worshipped in this way, without slapping on the label "liquid worship". Prayer occasions have been held in this style, too.

> In 2003, St Mary's Church, Luton held their three-hour Good Friday service in liquid mode. It was entitled "Holy Space". They had 15 zones – "Renew baptism vows", "Share a meal", "Triumphal entry to Jerusalem", "Thirst for Jesus", "Prayer for the world", "Gethsemane experience", "Journey to the cross", "Confess and forgive", "Prayer ministry" and several others. People moved through the zones at their own pace, and came together at the end for a final act of worship. Attendance soared from the normal 50 to over 270 from a range of backgrounds, young and old, regular churchgoers and people off the streets. For one visitor, it was a giant step into faith.

Liquid worship is based on the principles of emerging church. It offers alternatives in fluid form. It can draw together different ages, different backgrounds and people with different experiences more easily than traditional, one-size-fits-all worship. It could help culturally specific forms of church to intermingle with each other. Tailor-made church need not become "apartheid" church.

After a seminar on liquid worship at one of the St John's, Nottingham's "Fit for heaven" conferences, someone thanked me for giving the session on all-age worship! He had a point.

Cosy circles

A hallmark of consumer society is how middle-sized communities are on the way out. Friendships are replacing larger groups.

"Hubbing" not clubbing

Professor Sasha Roseneil of Leeds University has studied friendship in three different areas of Britain. Her results showed that "increasingly it is friendship that really matters in people's lives . . . Jools, a 28 year old heterosexual woman from an ex-mining town speaks for many people in 21st century Britain when she says: 'I think a friendship is for life, but I don't think a partner is . . . I'd marry my friends. They'd last longer.' "[3]

Fewer people are active in the branches of trade unions, political parties, the church and other traditional bodies. Members of new organisations, like environmental groups, tend to participate through a credit card or a website discussion rather than by turning up at meetings.[4] Involvement in groups of perhaps 20 to 30 people upward is giving way to small groups of friends, or one-to-one chats. A "friendly society" is taking on new meaning.

One reason is that choice is easing out long-term commitment – "I don't want to be tied down." A spontaneous meeting with friends feels more comfortable than a meeting arranged by someone else, at a time set well in advance. Most largish groups yield their rewards if you attend regularly, and that sits uneasily with an ethos of "I'll take it as it comes".

In the "blur" society, so many events compress into a day that they merge together. People complain that they have too much to do. The result? They sample one activity after another rather than commit to one or two. That way, they can dip into all the options.[5]

This sampling platform for life sabotages commitment to larger groups. "There are so many possibilities, I'll focus on people and activities that give me greatest satisfaction." Individuals spend time with people they are closest to and whom they most want to see.

Mobile phones and other modern communications are giving this a further twist. People can "grapevine" with close friends by text throughout the day. At the same time, they can click through Net-based relationships with contacts miles away. Largish groups, where you recognise everyone, are acquainted with most but know only a few well, get squeezed out.

Everyone needs a someone

Does the withering of larger groups matter? Consider this:

- *It undermines belonging.* There is no larger entity to which you belong, which is there for you whatever happens to your friends and which can be like an extended family for you.

- *It damages inclusion.* There are fewer gatherings for people to join if they are new to an area, if they want to be with people but find it hard to make close friends or if they are lonely. Fewer bridges link the edge of society to the mainstream.

- *It weakens caring.* Sometimes an individual requires more support than close friends or associates can provide – someone needing mental health or long-term physical care, for instance. In a larger group, support can be spread round more people.

- *It erodes autonomy.* In today's society, networks are more vital for success than ever before. Who you know really counts – to make you aware of a job, to point you to a special deal, to recommend a plumber or to advise you about your computer. A larger group of acquaintances will increase and strengthen your networks.

- *It stunts personal growth.* Active involvement in a larger group may give you more chance to develop your gifts, and brings you alongside people you might not choose to be with. Working through your differences – sometimes conflict – can help you become more patient, generous, humble and tolerant. Frustration and conflict are the raw materials of personal growth – "he drives me nuts, but I'm learning to cope with him". Casting aside larger groups may limit your chance to grow as a person.

Death of the congregation?

Unwittingly, many inherited churches have colluded with this shift from middle-sized community to friendship. They have leapt on to the small group bandwagon at the very time friendships have shown middling communities the door. Groups that work well tend to become friendship groups, with a strong life of their own. Cell church is giving the trend a fillip by privileging the role of small groups.

Small groups have mushroomed just as traditional congregations have lost their shine. Many people find church services formal and hierarchical when society has become informal and suspicious of authority.

Not much personal interaction takes place in a typical church service. Individuals sit in rows, like blocks of wood, saying little to each other. They are "spoken at" through the sermon, with no chance to answer back. Real community only begins after the service, when individuals mingle as they leave church or over a cup of coffee. It is as if the service is the entertainment, and community happens once the entertainment is over. But the quality of the "entertainment" is often poor – an hour of tedium perhaps for ten minutes of fellowship.

> **Stuart Murray Williams writes:**
> *It will be interesting to see how many emerging churches will resist the lure of the monologue sermon – and for how long. New churches often start with more dialogue but soon revert to the default monologue practice that has dominated the church since the fourth century. And some of them regard as radical sermons that are 75% longer than in "traditional" churches!*

I am astonished by the number of Christians who tell me how boring their church is, by which they mean Sunday worship. Some Christians have so despaired of the congregation that they have left church altogether.[6] Others find that their real church home is the small group. The congregation may feel dead, but small groups are very much alive.

Small groups have brought huge benefits to their members and infused new life into continuing church. Yet they are too small to perform the function of middle-sized communities. They can become so tight-knit that outsiders find it hard to break in. Members certainly care for each other, but if two of three need support the group's resources may be too small and narrow: a larger group is more likely to provide specialist help –

someone with the time to drive Barbara to hospital, for example.

Church members who don't belong to small groups may fall through the net. The networks represented by a little group will not be as extensive as in a bigger one. Cosy groups give individuals fewer opportunities to rub against "the awkward customer" than larger gatherings.

The inherited church has mimicked the society-wide shift from community to friendship, and risks the same harmful results.

Can emerging church do better?

Many fresh expressions of church are deliberately small-scale – meal-based meetings in a home for instance. Some pioneers have adopted cell-church principles, without bothering too much about bringing the cells into larger gatherings. Is emerging church about to join the flight from medium-sized communities?

Or will some fresh expressions, which are small now only because they are at an early stage, take root, grow and evolve into bigger gatherings (perhaps with small groups alongside)? Some church experiments are trying to make their gatherings more informal, with a stronger sense of community. Café churches, for example, can be highly interactive.

> So too is the Friary Drop-In, Nottingham. It was started by the Friary United Reformed Church in 1988 to provide support, advice and friendship to people whose lives were vulnerable to loss of work, health, housing, social and family ties, and personal confidence. The Drop-In is open three mornings a week, with 100 to 130 people of all ages at each session. In the mid 1990s a small congregation was started on Sunday evenings, which has grown to about 30. "You wouldn't get away with a sermon", someone told me. "They would interrupt you within the first couple of minutes." The congregation is highly informal, more like a large house group.

Liquid worship may be another way to loosen up the larger gathering. No more sitting in lines. Individuals can chat to each other as they move from one zone to another.

Will more relational and contemporary forms of congregation arise – a prophetic statement to a society that puts friendships above the wider group? Or will the larger gathering have currency in only some parts of society?

Satisfy society

Obesity has become headline news. Individuals are stuffing themselves with "inconvenience foods", not taking enough exercise and getting ill. "Feed me! Feed me!" is a powerful image of today's culture. Consumers push buttons and ask to be gratified.

Can emerging church challenge not only the "menumindset" and "cosy circles", but this "satisfy-me" mentality as well?

"Give me what I want"

The "satisfy society" reflects a provider-user model of consumerism. Power in the shopping mall has shifted toward the consumer. Shoppers now make their demands and suppliers dance to the customer tune. "Globalisation", which is locking countries together, has increased business competition. As companies jostle for position, they slash prices (many "white" goods are cheaper today – after inflation – than they were in the late 1980s), improve quality and personalise their offerings.

When you get a hotel for music lovers, or customised perfumes give a new meaning to dollars and scents, or a car rolls off the assembly line tagged for a specific owner, or children can have their name written into a story line, you know that the new personalised world has emphatically arrived.

Choice is growing exponentially, so much so that "option paralysis" is reaching epidemic proportions. Increasingly "shopped out" consumers are thinking, "Don't give me more choice. I've got too much as it is. Just give me what I want." "I want what I want" is beginning to emerge as the new consumer ethic. Customer expectations are hitting the stratosphere.[7]

The passive consumer

"I want what I want" is combining with "Satisfy me! Satisfy me!" to produce the passive consumer. Consumers issue their demands, hold out their credit cards and wait to be fed with the products they fancy.

In some walks of life, the passive consumer is a real problem. Take healthcare: professionals are desperate for patients to feel responsible for their health rather than relying exclusively on the doctor. Many pill-stuffed patients might not have been ill at all if they had adopted preventive strategies. Likewise, modest pupils can shine when they become partners in their learning instead of being spoon-fed by their teachers. Crime is best tackled when citizens cooperate with the police.

Current thinking about public sector reform is starting to move beyond the mantra "expand choice" to the concept of "co-production". Users and providers would work together to create public services and improve outcomes. The language of "delivery" is being challenged by the concept of shared responsibility.[8]

Passive churchgoers

"Satisfy me! Satisfy me!" is no stranger to inherited church! More and more worshippers demand to be entertained and are dissatisfied if they are not. A recent *Washington Post* article quoted a US pastor: "Worship is a form of entertainment . . . If people are not entertained, they don't feel they are participating."[9] Is Hollywood church coming to town?

Inherited churches have often allowed Christians to depend on entertaining worship, or the sermon, or the sacraments, or the minister for their spiritual well-being. Nothing wrong with that, you may think. The church is meant to feed believers through worship, preaching and mutual give and take.

The trouble is that it has often bred an over-dependency. The minister leaves and a virus called pastoral crisis devastates the congregation – "We'll never cope!" Parents outsource the spiritual formation of their children to Sunday school or the youth club. Not taught to pray, read the Bible, promote justice and care for creation, the children grow up with a faith disconnect: belief is not part of their everyday lives.

Or adults get spiritual fill-ups on Sunday and perhaps in a small group, but do little to grow their faith in between. Their spiritual health becomes the church's responsibility, not something for which they also carry the can. When things go wrong, they blame the church.

A different tack?

Some fresh expressions of church have yet to challenge the satisfy-me ethos. They perpetuate a provider-user model of church. Might this be the future? Will emerging churches use technology to replicate the entertainment-based worship found in the mainstream? Will video sermons by superstar preachers be downloaded from the Net, creating new forms of dependency? Might presentational videos, splicing material from different websites, encourage spectator congregations?

Or will emerging churches operate in a different vein? Some are exploring more interactive styles of worship, both to foster community and avoid over-dependency. Some café churches, for instance, have a short introduction to a topic and encourage people to discuss it, while sitting at their tables. Liquid worship may be another way in to more interactive gatherings – a prayer zone where each person can add a stanza in a collective poem to God, for example.

When I described to my colleagues one such gathering, which had been interactive from beginning to end, some exclaimed "How exhausting!" Not everyone finds that form of worship helpful. But there are myriad other ways to avoid provider-user church.

Within emerging church circles (and outside) there is growing interest in reflective worship, accenting stillness for example. In a busy, busy world, people often value oases of space. Quietly meditating on Scripture, perhaps in a guided form, can be just as demanding as a discussion, but feel different. It could be another way to share the responsibility for spiritual sustenance.

> *George Lings writes:*
> *It is interesting how many of the practical examples Mike gives in the book are mainly to do with how* meetings for worship *can be done differently. So often worship becomes the most valued dimension of being church. I'd want to balance that by more cases that explore how the other church dimensions of* community *and* mission *can be expressed differently, but in ways that fit the contexts those churches face. I'd even argue that the best worship grows out of authentic community and genuine mission. It's actually last, not first, in the process of growing church.*

St Thomas Crookes, Sheffield, actively encourages parents to share responsibility for their children's spiritual development. It says to parents, "The spiritual health of children is not our responsibility, but yours. We'll equip you through training courses to help your children mature in the faith, we'll provide you with material to use at home with the family, and we shall support what you do through our children's and young people's activities at church. But we are not taking the responsibility ourselves. Our task is to resource you."

This is a deliberate attempt to get away from a provider-client model of church. Other churches may feel that they are too small to support their parents in this way. But why not offer training courses and children's activities jointly with other churches in the area?

Australians Michael Frost and Alan Hirsch have written about mission action as a sacrament – not activism for the sake of it, but deeds that "actually confer grace" through the alleviation of poverty and other mission activity.[10] Christians have to be active if church is to be mission-shaped. This is the opposite of a dependency-based passivity. Will fresh expressions create a culture in which churchgoers take responsibility for their own involvement in active mission?

Me-mould

Consumer values are often "me" centred – "Satisfy me!", "I want what I want" or "It must fit me exactly". The inherited church has often colluded with this. Many believers have embraced a self-focused gospel – "I am the object of the cross", "God loves me", "My worship experience is important" or "It's my healing that counts". Faith becomes all about me rather than about glorifying God and serving other people. Partly this reflects today's culture, which has clasped the church warmly by the throat.

Me-spirituality

Perhaps it also reflects, at least in the evangelical tradition, priorities within the church. After the Second World War some Christian leaders believed that the church contained too many people who attended periodically, shared Christian values but had not encountered God in a personal way. Much evangelism aimed to encourage them, in the cliché of the day, to move from "churchianity" to Christianity.

Then came the Charismatic and other renewal movements, which – alongside the Pentecostal movement – sought to deepen personal faith through a more powerful experience of the Holy Spirit. Intimacy with God through worship or the spiritual disciplines became a priority.

Some leaders of renewal, such as John Wimber, explicitly cast their theology in a Kingdom framework: renewal was to equip the church to help transform the world. Yet despite this, many Christians came into renewal through personal experience rather than social engagement. Resourcing church members loomed larger than changing society. "My relationship with God" became all-important, with justice and the environment as spiritual add-ons.

In a me-first culture, the result was lethal. Believers slipped into a self-oriented spirituality – compare the number of retreats and conferences on topics like prayer with the number addressing social issues! Much of the inherited church remains

lethargic in the face of injustice and the destruction of creation. Personal encounters with God are ends in themselves rather than the fuel for Kingdom change.[11]

> Steve Gee, a church planter within the Vineyard stream of churches, blogged a reflection on whether churches "just help us warehouse Christians till they die"? He blamed a Gospel of Sin Management:
>
>> Jesus died for our sin and we'll go to heaven when we die. But what if heaven isn't the goal of God's story, what if it is just our destination? What if the goal of the gospel (salvation, Christ dying for our sin, etc) was something else? What if the goal was more about life than death . . . about the start of a whole new life? A kingdom kind of life? . . .
>>
>> Perhaps our evangelistic question should change from "If you were going to die tonight, do you know where you would go?" to "If you were going to live tomorrow (and live for a very long time), whom would you live for? What would you do? What is the basic and fundamental story around which you would live your life?"

Radical roots

One fear about emerging church is that it will mirror these me-first consumer values, just like the inherited church. Some people ask, "Doesn't alternative church make so many concessions to the it-must-fit-me world that it surrenders to a toxic individualism? Worse still, if each person finds an expression of church in their own image, might they not create God in their image too – a 'designer church' peddling 'designer spirituality'? Can emerging church really subvert the me-society?"

Though it is too early to know, some hopeful straws are quivering. First, a church "that fits me" is not the only value of emerging church: more radical ones exist too – transformation for example, as we saw in the second chapter. Core to emerging church is being immersed in a group's culture to help others, if they wish, encounter the God of change. Fitting other people takes priority over "it must fit me".

Sacrifice is another value – giving up my preconception of church to allow a more suitable expression to emerge.

Reproduction speaks of stepping out of my comfort zone to plant a further expression of church. Respecting diversity means accepting another group's cultural preferences instead of imposing my own. The vision for unity means embracing people who are different, when I might rather not.

These values are notes in a different tune to consumer selfishness. Can they remain dominant, once new expressions of church are well established?

Hope in desperation

A second "straw" is that conditions in parts of Western society may favour radically new forms of Christian community. One group of ministers remarked, "In our city, churches are so small that we *have* to do emerging church. It only takes us one or two days a week to look after our existing congregations. What else would we do if we didn't get involved with the community?" The smallness of church has created space to serve those who don't come to church.

Community development provides a vintage opportunity to experiment with less pietistic models of church. As Christians work with single parents, groups of older people, disaffected youngsters or those with addictions, individuals may be drawn into communities of service before they are drawn into faith.

They will encounter Christ when they are served by other people. They may also experience something of the mutual love within the Trinity when they serve each other – perhaps through a support group. So if they come to engage with Christ explicitly, it will be in the context of an outward movement of love. They will be formed as Christians in the context of service, with worship as a related dimension. Might this be rather different to being formed primarily in the context of worship?

"Urban Expression recruits, equips, deploys and supports self-financing teams to pioneer innovative and relevant expressions of the Christian Church in under-churched areas of the inner city." One of its first teams has become Cable Street Community Church in

Shadwell, East London.

From tiny beginnings, it now meets in three households on a Sunday, and altogether on Wednesday evenings. Seven years since it began, it is now learning to "adjust to being a larger church".[12] Might Cable Street be a fragment of the twenty-first century church that somehow got dropped into the twentieth century?

"Urban Expression has always been rooted in core values," which "undergird all we do." The values include:

- "We believe that the gospel works through relationships and that serving God consists largely in building life-giving relationships with others."
- "We focus on under-churched areas and neglected people, trying to find ways of communicating Jesus appropriately to those most frequently marginalized, condemned and abused by society."
- "We challenge the trend of some Christians moving out of the cities and encourage Christians to relocate to the inner cities."
- "We realise the importance of living uncluttered lives, holding possessions lightly and recognising that all we have is to be at God's disposal."

Prizing these and other values has encouraged expressions of church that are committed to "unconditional service, holistic mission, bold proclamation, prioritising the poor and being a voice for the voiceless". That is the type of community that visitors, seekers and newcomers experience. Values, taught and applied, are key. Those who journey into faith have their expectations shaped by communities with a radical edge.

Just as the early years are crucial for an individual's later development, so how people are brought into faith has a lasting impact. Will those born into faith through community engagement remain eager to serve the wider world? Or as so often in the inherited church, will they grow tired, hit the snooze button and go contentedly to sleep?

Travelling light

A third reason to hope that emerging church can challenge the "me-society" is that some fresh expressions of church are seeking to throw off the excess baggage of church, freeing up members to serve the outside community. It is amazing how complicated church has become!

In some traditions, a Sunday morning service will require the band or choir to have practised, the OHP (or PowerPoint projector) to have been set up, acetates to have been rooted out of the box in the right order (or the computer programmed), the microphones to have been checked, crèche helpers to have turned up, all the children's groups to have the right material and the leaders to be prepared, the preacher to be ready, those leading the prayers to have remembered, the readings to have been selected and those reading to have been notified, the banner group to have found a way of hanging their banner, differences about what should be in the service to have been negotiated . . . And all this, not just once a month, but weekly!

Look at what is involved in "servicing the service", then add in church during the rest of the week and think of all the energy required! Is it surprising that many people have little time for mission? Church ends up as a parallel world.

A number of emerging churches are trying to make it simple. Some ask, "Does a congregation have to meet every week? If our small groups meet regularly, why not have an 'all together' service just twice a month?" Others are saying, "Let's meet over a meal. We can take over a café, or take it in turns to cook or each bring a dish. Then let the conversation flow, with prayer and Bible study as appropriate."

One couple described a twice-monthly gathering they led on Sunday afternoons. "We don't even think about it till Friday evening. Everything is kept as simple as possible – a few notices, a warm-up activity to get people talking, breaking down into smaller groups and inviting groups to discuss a Bible passage. All we have to do is to plan the warm-up and the topic for discussion."

Will "simple church" become the norm? And if so, will it free up individuals and churches to dance with the world outside, celebrating life, standing alongside those who hurt and loving people into faith?[13]

A re-think

Finally, as we saw in Chapter Two, more and more Christians in emerging church circles are looking again at the versions of the faith they have imbibed – read the numerous blogs on the emerging church websites![14] They are discovering that salvation is more than something we receive: it is something we participate in. Our lives get caught up in a movement much bigger than ourselves – in God's change programme for society.

Taking a fresh look at the church has encouraged a fresh look at the gospel. This creates a chance to shift from an individualistic to a more rounded, self-giving faith. How many new expressions of church will hang out the sign, "Warning! Church could damage your comfort zone"?

Fresh expressions, a fresh start?

It is easy to be over-critical of our consumer society. It contains much to celebrate – new ways to experience the material world, opportunities to party and have fun, the chance to look good and be creative, a staggering array of means to express oneself and be fulfilled, and entertainment to suit almost every taste.

But the consumer world has a price tag. It privileges the affluent and excludes the poor. It has harmed the environment and championed choice at the expense of other, sometimes more important values. It can lead to hedonistic lifestyles that downplay moral obligations and appeal to the baser instincts.

Will emerging church elevate the consumer at the expense of poor people? Not necessarily. It has the potential – perhaps more than inherited church – to protect "civic values". These values are essential to safeguard the interests of the poor.

Increasingly individuals behave as consumers in the public realm. Electors vote on the basis of how they will benefit as individuals rather than what is best for the public good. Votes become an expression of consumer power – "Which party will deliver the best public services to me?"[15]

This erodes the notion that each individual's well-being is bound up with the welfare of others. As a middle-class person, for example, I benefit too when resources are devoted to tackling poverty or protecting the health of those on the social margins. These measures will create a more prosperous and inclusive society, in which the tax burden can be more widely shared, for instance.

This sense of being tied in with other people is a profoundly biblical theme. It lies, for example, behind many of the Old Testament injunctions to protect the disadvantaged.

Might emerging church create moral communities that bind their members to the welfare of society? And might this commitment check, modestly, the cultural drift to individualism at the expense of those who are left behind? The answer could be a resounding "Yes", but only if emerging church can realise its potential to counter the "menu mindset", "cosy circles", "satisfy society" and "me mould".

Believers might then be shaped by Christian communities which model "civic values" alongside consumer ones. They might experience more diverse and inclusive expressions of church. They might be active rather than passive consumers of spirituality, perhaps encouraging a more active engagement with society.[16] They might belong to churches that become radical itches within the me-world.

Notes

1. For an example, see Michael Moynagh, *Changing World, Changing Church*, Monarch, 2001, p. 159.
2. Pete Ward gives some examples in *Liquid Church*, Carlisle: Paternoster, 2002, pp. 94–97. The concept has been written up by Tim Lomax, *More Freedom within a Framework*, Stowmarket: Kevin Mayhew, 2002, pp. 14–15, 124–28. Tim and I will be writing at greater length about this, with prac-

tical suggestions, in the months ahead.

3. Sasha Roseneil, "Towards a more friendly society?", *The Edge*, 15, March 2004, p. 12.

4. Performance and Innovation Unit, *Social Capital: A discussion paper*, London: Cabinet Office, 2002, pp. 34–39.

5. For example, in the late 1990s more than twice as many people in the UK had access to a bicycle as they did twenty years before. Yet on average those bicycles covered just a third of the distance (*Forestry Futures: Drivers for Change in Rural Recreation*, A report to the Forestry Commission by the Future Foundation, 1998, pp. 10–11).

6. A number of the people interviewed by Alan Jamieson spoke of how their spirituality was drying up in the existing congregations. There were many reasons for this, but the lack of real community was almost certainly a factor. See, for example, Alan Jamieson, *A Churchless Faith*, London: SPCK, 2002, p. 34.

7. These themes are discussed more fully in Michael Moynagh, *Changing World, Changing Church*, London: Monarch, 2001, Chapters Two and Three.

8. See for example, Tom Bentley and James Wilsdon, "Introduction: the adaptive state" in Tom Bentley and James Wilsdon (eds), *The Adaptive State: Strategies for personalising the public sector*, London: Demos, 2003, pp. 13–36.

9. "Churches Turn up Volume with Big Sound Systems", *Washington Post*, 5 January 2003.

10. Michael Frost and Alan Hirsch, *The Shaping of Things to Come*, Peabody: Hendrickson, 2003, Chapter Eight.

11. The dangers of this are a major theme of contemporary theology from all the traditions. One helpful treatment is Tom Wright, *New Tasks for a Renewed Church*, London: Hodder & Stoughton, 1992.

12. Urban Expression Newsletter, February 2004.

13. It has been interesting to find that Stuart Murray has also written about "simple church" (in *Post-Christendom*,

Carlisle: Paternoster, 2004, pp. 274–76); we both came to it separately.

14. See, for example, some of the links from www.emergent-uk.org and www.opensourcetheology.net.

15. A striking example in the UK's 2001 general election was electors in Kidderminster voting for the candidate who would campaign to keep their local hospital open. The more pervasive example is the competition between political parties to convince voters that each can deliver better public services than its rivals.

16. Robert Wuthnow, for example, found that being involved in small groups encouraged American Christians to be more active in their local communities. See Chapter Six.

CHAPTER SIX

CHURCH! GET ME OUT OF HERE!

"Church feels so regimented!" a young couple complained. Their despair barometer soared as they described how hemmed in they felt. Their church appealed strongly to their age group, but seemed shackled by leg-iron views of what church should be like. "If only we could be more imaginative and flexible!"

Emerging church can set people free. It challenges straitjacket thinking about church. It throws up questions like: "What is church?" "How important is it for Christians to meet together?" "Does the size of gathering matter?" "What links, if any, should a Christian group have to the wider church?" "Does the dawning age of 'liquid' church rub place off the map?" "Can't we ditch terms like 'congregation' and 'church' anyway?"

Exploring these questions opens the box. It puts on the table different ways of imagining church. It can reshuffle the mental furniture, spark fresh ideas and catalyse new vision. It can give Christians permission to experiment and be creative. The questions have no steel-case answers. Nor do they invite anything goes. Variety can reign within a broad framework. Key elements of that framework are the outward and homeward movements of the Holy Spirit.

The journeys of the Spirit

A little girl was crying on the beach. Two boys were playing catch, while she looked on. Then one of the boys threw her the ball. She threw it back. Through her tears came a smile of Hollywood wattage: she was now part of the game.

Recent theologians have taken a renewed interest in the Trinity.[1] They have discovered a fresh emphasis on God's invitation to believers to participate in the life of the Trinity. Believers are not "over here" while God is "over there". They are welcomed into the corporate life of the Father, Son and Holy Spirit, just as the girl was drawn into the game.

Individuals are drawn into the life of God as they pray, for example. Christians pray in the power of the Spirit and in the name of the Son, who intercedes with the Father on their behalf. It is as if their prayer gets caught up in the eternal conversation between the three persons who comprise God.

Church, as the body of Christ, is an important way that individuals participate in God. It is a visible expression of their welcome into the collective life of the Trinity, making it in a profound sense God's family.

The Holy Spirit adopts individuals into that family through a constant outward and homeward "journey". The Spirit is sent by the Father and the Son on an "outward journey" to a broken world. Men and women are then drawn toward the Godhead as part of the Spirit's "homeward journey", as it were.

Jesus modelled these movements himself. He went out from the Father and formed a community of disciples. He then drew that community toward the Father, teaching his followers to use the intimate term, "Abba". The Spirit continues the Son's work.

These two movements, continually back and forth, are the pulse of the church. The Spirit's journey to the world is a mission to bring the Christian community into existence. The Spirit's journey home begins to shape that community in God's likeness.

Proper church?

One, rather basic question raised by emerging church is what do we actually mean by "church".

Some fresh expressions, for example, are greeted with the complaint, "It's not that church is no longer what it used to be. It's worse! Church has stopped being church at all!" Holy Communion may look like high tea. Sunday worship may have disappeared (to another day of the week perhaps). Meetings may be irregular. Where's the sermon? "You call this church?" "It's no more church than Mickey is a mouse!"

Some pioneers of emerging church feel disillusioned with the mainstream. Much of their energy comes from a passion to express church more authentically. Initially they may define church by what it is not – "It's not top-down leadership, boxed-in conformity and heavy-weight expectations."

But they cannot go on defining church in negative terms. After a while, they need a positive view: not what church isn't, but what it is. What is at the heart of church? What kind of Christian community should they be trying to create? As people are drawn into the faith, what would be authentic church for them?

It all depends?

So what's the irreducible minimum to be church? What would be revealed if church did the Full Monty? Answers are as varied as the traditions within church. Some Christians would be minimalist – "Church is any community of believers in Christ indwelt by the Spirit." Others ask what that means in practice.

What are the signs that the Spirit indwells a community? Is it proclamation of the Word? The sacraments? Is it the Ephesians 4 ministries – apostleship, prophecy, evangelism, pastoral care and teaching? Is it mission? Is it Christian service? Or is it a combination of these?

Any definition of church risks being too vague to be meaningful, or too specific to be inclusive: "You're not church because you don't do certain things." Different expressions of church may not be welcomed within the body because "they don't do it right".

Whose shape?

A middle course might highlight the outward and homeward movements of the Spirit. These movements were revealed at Pentecost when the Spirit went out to Jerusalem. The Spirit then drew 3,000 new believers toward the Father and the Son, inspiring them to become more like Christ.

These outward and homeward movements have been repeated ever since. Whenever the church has gone out to others and helped them draw closer to God, it has travelled with the Spirit out to the fallen world and homeward toward the Godhead.

Recognising these movements can keep a balance between two emphases. Some in the emerging church corner stress the outward movement of the Spirit in mission. Church should be shaped by its mission context.

Others in the "correct doctrine" corner say that this allows the church to be over-shaped by its surrounding culture. They stress, in effect, the homeward journey of the Spirit. The Spirit is drawing the church toward its destination, unity with Christ in heaven. This vision of what it will one day become should fashion the church now.

Each of these emphases, of course, is crucial. Both the outward and the homeward movements of the Spirit form church. Church is not mission-shaped alone, nor just heavenly-moulded. It is the two together: a mission-shaped church being prepared for heaven, and living out that future today.

George Lings writes:
I think Mike has helpfully connected two motivations that should never have been allowed to drift apart. Church is both the consequence of history – that Jesus came, did his unique work and told us to continue his mission (John

20:21) – and church is also to respond to the Holy Spirit
(Acts 1:8), who makes the future visible in the present and
brings a foretaste of the future's values.

Count everyone in?

This double movement of the Spirit has implications for inclusiveness: how can church be splendidly inclusive of non-believers, yet retain its identity in Christ?

Many pioneers of emerging church groan at the idea of strict
membership criteria. They fear that rigid boundaries will
produce a "them and us" attitude, which cuts church off from
non-believers. They prefer an "open source" church, which
crashes through the boundaries between one person and
another.

The danger with openness is that if everyone belongs to the
church whatever they believe, the group could lose its Christian
distinctiveness. Equally, if the church becomes a radical, gathered community, it might degenerate into a self-selected ginger
group and exclude others.

The work of the Spirit offers a pattern for holding openness
and distinctiveness together. The Spirit's outward journey is to
everyone in the world, and the Spirit's homeward movement is
to draw individuals toward the Godhead.

The early Christians expressed this by gathering together for
a full meal, to which everyone was invited. They would chat
about everyday life, and perhaps include a talk about Jesus.
Then those who were baptised in the name of the Lord would
progress to a second stage. They would take the leftover bread
and wine, and celebrate them as an ante-past of the Messianic
banquet to come. All were included in the evening, without
threatening the Christian community's distinctiveness.[2]

Emerging church often does the same sort of thing – an arts
project open to everyone for instance, but with an invitation to
join a spiritual exploration group; or social events that can be
stepping stones into an *Alpha* or *Start* course for those interested.

A Baptist church in Bracknell holds "out" and "in" together rather differently, by hosting a Sunday congregation in a leisure centre. The Sunday newspapers are available, so is plenty of coffee and the chairs are comfortable. Over the two-hour period, there might be 50 minutes of chat-show interviews, comment and discussion about topical issues, a multimedia presentation possibly and perhaps the presentation of some music. People can listen, talk quietly or read the papers. When the presentation starts, the men often disappear behind their papers – but listen surreptitiously! Some stay on afterwards for lunch or to use the leisure facilities. People with no Christian commitment can feel at home, but there is a specifically Christian dimension.

In, up, of and out

After the Spirit's outward movement to bring the church into existence, the Spirit leads the church on a homeward journey toward God. What does this homeward movement entail? George Lings helpfully talks about four core dimensions to church.[3]

- An "up" dimension towards God. As the community reaches up to God in sacramental, word-based or other forms of worship, God comes "down" to transform individuals' lives and make them more like him in character.
- An "in" dimension, as the community fosters high quality relationships between its members. The community seeks to become inclusive, like the Trinity, with room for everyone.
- An "out" dimension. The community goes out to the world to care for it and redeem it. Evangelism is one aspect of holistic mission. Just as the Spirit constantly moves out to the world and in towards the Godhead, so does the church.
- An "of" dimension, as each community identifies with the whole church – "We are part of the church flowing through history, lapping round the world today and rushing forward to eternity." Might this also be an "around" dimension, as Christian communities look around to make links with their wider family?

These ingredients were the signature of the New Testament church. They have been reflected down the ages in the church's confession that it should be one (the "in" dimension), holy ("up"), catholic ("of") and apostolic ("out").[4] They remain the essence of church today.

Held together, these elements will give *definition* to emerging church. One woman described a community centre she managed. "We care for people. We show them respect. I pray for individuals. We don't hold worship services, but it's still church!" True?

Perhaps her centre was the beginning of church. She had engaged in an "out" movement to the world, but some of the other dimensions of church had yet to develop – "up" in worship and "of" in a conscious belonging to the whole body of Christ. Clarity about the meaning of church will save us from being drowned in an ocean of vagueness.

'Up", "in", "out" and "of" give *direction* to emerging church. That particular community centre was certainly *an* expression of church. But how might it become a fuller expression? Other new forms of church may face a similar question. They may have "up" and "in" dimensions, for example, but do they have a sense of "of"? Are they moving "out"? Here is a vision for emerging church: to keep growing in all four directions.

Free to explore

These four dimensions also give *discretion* to emerging church. What does it mean to have an "up", "in", "out" and "of" community life? Answers will be found by reflecting on Scripture and the insights of other Christians. Inevitably, conclusions will vary.

Sticking to a four-dimensional, bare-bones definition of church will focus on what is really important. If Christians make a fuller description of each dimension fundamental to the church, they will fall out over the detail – "That's not proper church if you do it like that!"

Getting hung up on the specifics of one dimension risks

undermining the others. You may be wonderfully correct about the details of "up" and "out", but insisting that other expressions of church share the same view may provoke disputes that wreck "in" or "of". The tiniest wrinkles are removed from one part of the body, while key bones in the skeleton are allowed to crumble. One overseas mission agency reports getting promises of financial support provided none of its staff use *Alpha*!

So it will be unhelpful to nail down emerging Christian groups with detailed prescriptions: "You must celebrate Holy Communion in this way", "Mission equals *Alpha* or *Christianity Explored*" or "'of' means a United Service". Groups should have plenty of scope to write their own scripts as they pray, study the Bible and allow the Spirit to lead them. "Why can't church be more flexible?" Take a "Get out of Jail" card: it can.

Solid, liquid – or gas?

"I was fed up with Christians and congregations, fed up of me and my friends being let down by people who didn't (want to?) understand," recalls Anna Dodridge, Advice Worker for Bournemouth University Student Union:

So I gave up . . . and I found other people fed up, other people who had no home, people who never had a hope in the first place – believers with no body.

So now we hang out together, like I do with any of my friends. We are families, kids, grown-ups, wrinklies, wisdom and experience, youth and enthusiasm, intellectual and hasty, crappy and forgiven. People I never thought I would have anything much to speak about with are my family.

And that's it. No alt.services, no small group meetings. We just get on with our lives. We pray together, we give and receive prophecy, we worship God in service actions and conversations, we hear and teach the Bible by our everyday conversations and circumstances. We eat together and communion as a fellowship of friends. We share, we are accountable . . .

We have a wider context in our area. We get together with the people from around who are doing the same thing . . . It's really all about the way we live together as Christians, and that's it. We have committed ourselves to each other, looking out for each other in prayer and that's that. As long as we get together regularly and something useful towards us getting to know Jesus happens, we've been church.[5]

Liquid communities

A growing number of people, like Anna, are "churching it" outside traditional structures, in a highly fluid way. They are posing a second question about church: in our more liquid society, do we need the same-people-in-the-same-place gathering that is so strong a feature of the inherited church?

Pete Ward has suggested that we should dethrone the weekly congregation. Church can exist as much in the networks that people create as in a weekly meeting. What counts is not the form that community takes, such as a fixed gathering once a week, but the existence of community, whatever its form.[6]

A weekly meeting may well be too rigid for many people in our fluid world. Individuals working shifts or with weekend family commitments cannot easily be tied down to a weekly event. One-hour church in a 24/7 society does not work.

Other people express community not by sitting in rows, facing the front and ignoring the person alongside, but by spontaneously getting together with friends, texting them and keeping in touch on-line. They find liquid expressions of church more authentic than solid, traditional versions.

Against this are fears that liquid church may evaporate into gas. Might relationships be too transient to create real commitment? Gatherings may be too infrequent to build up the body. Fluid encounters with two or three people may be no substitute for the sense of God's presence generated by worshippers together. "Tacit" learning, like noticing how others behave, may suffer if individuals meet intermittently. Sacramental worship may be neglected. The pastoral needs of people on the edge are more likely to be picked up through regular meetings than periodic encounters.

Flexi-church

The outward and homeward journeys of the Spirit, once again, can help us navigate through this debate. As the Spirit goes out to a damaged world and becomes immersed in different cultures, expressions of church must be expressed realistically within those cultures.

There is little point in having a culturally alien pattern of church. Newcomers will struggle to get involved, while existing members may leave because the church is such hard work. So if the culture warms to regular gatherings, a solid expression of church will be appropriate. But if people live more fluid lives, the church may need to be more flexible too.

At the same time, the Spirit's journey home is a movement toward community. The Spirit draws believers into the divine community of Father, Son and Holy Spirit. In this community all are made one in Christ. As believers accompany the Spirit on that journey, they will seek expressions of community that match their destination.

So however fixed or fluid church may be, a key question will be whether it promotes Christian community. A weekly congregation does not guarantee a community: individuals may remain strangers. Nor does a liquid expression of church: being authentically spontaneous can leave some people out. What counts is the commitment of individuals to one another.

George Lings writes:

Our research work on fresh expressions of church, not least those starting to reach people furthest away from the existing church, has found this to be the single most important lesson we have learnt. Until outsiders see in the communal lives of Christians something they admire, almost nothing else can happen. It is also true for more and more Christians that in the end quality community is what keeps them going, more than cool worship or exciting mission.

Many Christians would also want to emphasise the importance of gatherings to celebrate the sacraments, particularly Holy Communion, which can play an important role in building community. Can you really take Communion down a wire?

Being culturally realistic and creating community are obviously linked. You can't build community if it does not work. What will work in most cases will be a mixture of gatherings and networks, but the balance will increasingly vary.

Liquid church can say to solid church, "How active are your networks between meetings? Are you using them to strengthen community?" Solid church can ask of liquid church, "How often are you drawing people together, using face-to-face gatherings to underpin community?" Differences can be a chance to learn from one another.

> **Stuart Murray Williams writes:**
> *Hope for the future of the church in Western culture does not lie with the inherited church. Nor does it lie with the emerging church. It lies in conversations between inherited and emerging churches that enable each to learn from the other and together find fresh ways of incarnating the gospel in a changing and diverse culture.*

So, "this is how we have always done it"? The church can get that monkey off its back! You don't have to meet weekly. Nor do you have to load everything on to the gathering. Other ways of expressing church may fit the context better. Emerging church is a call not to be tied to the past, but to strain toward new forms of Christian community – communities throbbing with the love of Christ.

Should congregations cell out?

Emerging church shuffles a third deck of cards: if face-to-face meetings are desirable, do they need to take the form of a congregation? Can't we ditch congregations and have small groups instead?

This won't be a pressing question if the group is small, of course. But if numbers grow, should the aim be to multiply small groups and make them the centre of the church? Or should the groups be gathered into a congregation, which has a central role? This relates, clearly, to the issue of middle-sized communities discussed in the last chapter.

> "They are deliberately trying not to plant congregations", remarked one member of the Northumbria community. He described some of his community friends in different parts of the country. One couple invited their neighbours to collect leaves from the local parks to use as compost in their gardens. They then hosted an event on the theme of leaves, picking up "spiritual" issues such as growth, death and new life.
>
> Another couple turned the basement of their home into a prayer cellar, open to local residents at advertised times. Sometimes they have invited local people to pop in on a specific day to pray around a particular topic – a major news event perhaps. A third couple have held street parties.
>
> All three couples have turned their back on monolithic congregations. They want to encourage small-scale expressions of community, in which the Christian dimension has a chance to grow.

Do experiments like these herald the death of the congregation?

Turning church upside down

In an interview Bob and Mary Hopkins, who support and coach leaders of emerging church, recalled the first-century Jewish model of religious community – the extended household in which the Sabbath and Passover meals were celebrated and the Old Testament law was taught; the synagogue which comprised a fairly small number of households and was interactive in style; and the festival or pilgrimage (centred on the temple in Jerusalem), which was a much larger event.

This pattern was echoed in the medieval church and some expressions of church since, where the home was a place of family instruction and devotions, the congregation met regularly and simply in the local church, and periodically congregations gathered in the cathedral.

The trouble was that over the centuries, the traditional church fell away from the Jewish model, Bob and Mary suggested. Anglican parishes aped the cathedral. They tried to enact festival-type worship every week. Their robed and processing choirs imitated cathedral choirs, they developed ever more elaborate liturgies, the priest was put on a pedestal and formality ruled. This formality was appropriate in a cathedral setting, but helped to undermine community within the local church. As society became more relaxed, formality became even more of a problem.

Over the last 30 years small midweek groups have tried to recapture some of the missing sense of community. Cell church took this a giant step further by turning church on its head. Instead of the Sunday congregation being central, with midweek groups in support, weekly cells became the focus of church life.

Many cell advocates place such an emphasis on cell and celebration that the middle tier has been downplayed, often unwittingly. "Is it time to rehabilitate the congregation?" Bob and Mary asked.

Sharing the journey

American sociologist Robert Wuthnow has studied the small group movement in the United States. He found that small groups, mostly home-based, had certain advantages. They were culturally bespoke – individuals could find something that suited their taste, but move when their interests changed. Even so, most groups were relatively stable and their members committed; they were not "one-night stands".

Groups gave their members encouragement and support, allowed them to express their ideas openly and cultivated trust. Many involved were spiritually nourished, enjoyed close relationships and felt appreciated. Much to his surprise, Wuthnow found that small groups often prompted members to become more active in the community – as volunteers or by supporting community-wide activities.[7]

But small groups also had weaknesses. They could end up in a sub-Christian niche, comfortable but not open to fresh truths. They bred a do-it-yourself religion – belief in a God who makes life easier rather than fostering a sense of awe. They encouraged people to feel better about themselves, but were not so good at transforming their lifestyles.[8]

Wuthnow's findings reinforce arguments put forward in Chapter Five against relying too heavily on small groups: better perhaps a multi-layered approach, with a strong emphasis on each level – small group, larger gathering and the occasional celebration. The different layers can complement and support each other.

Multi-level

The middle tier, larger gatherings, should not be undervalued. In our splintering society, as we have seen, congregations of 30 to 80 people can provide communities small enough for individuals to feel they belong, but large enough to connect people who would otherwise be apart. They can rebuild middle-sized communities.

They are especially important for mobilising people. It will be much harder to develop a significantly sized "social concern" project if Christians meet mainly in small cells. You need a regular, larger gathering so that people can be encouraged to back the project at the beginning, receive regular reports about how it is getting on, see some of the people involved and have a sense that they are "in it" with a significant number of other Christians.

The two movements of the Spirit are very much about community. The Spirit moves out to connect with a fractured world. The church travels with the Spirit when it mobilises to serve that world. The Spirit also travels homeward, drawing the fragments of society into a final unity when the journey is complete. The church accompanies the Spirit by seeking ways of knitting society together in the here-and-now.

Many new expressions of church tend to be at the level of cell. This is inevitable as small groups tentatively feel their way toward authentic Christianity. Sustaining the group can be a challenge in itself, let alone build new layers on top! Yet it may help to have a vision of what emerging church might become – a pointer to how the church could evolve.

Gatherings of, say, 30 to 80 people would provide a healthy complement to small groups. They would provide a fuller expression of community than small groups alone. They might also help denominations with a shortage of priests, but require a priest to preside at Holy Communion: the gathering could be an occasion when Communion was celebrated with everyone together, and an opportunity perhaps to "reserve" the sacrament for small groups in the priest's absence.[9]

Gatherings might meet regularly, but not every week. They could be very different in style to traditional congregations – eschewing a "boxed" hymn sandwich or rigid liturgical approach, and being more like "cell" on a large plane.

St Thomas Crookes, Sheffield, provides an example on a massive scale. Cells meet perhaps twice a month, and then come together in regular (often fortnightly) clusters, though there is plenty of variation. Clusters tend to be based on a particular focus, such as the workplace or families. Meetings are simple – maybe notices to start with, a couple of songs listened to or sung and then a group activity. For example, "Joan has brought some un-iced cakes. There's icing in a bowl. If you would like, please take a cake, ice it, give it to someone you don't know well and talk about the sort of week you have both had. After that, you may want to link up with two other couples. If you have been reading the Bible, you might want to share what you have been reading or what you've been learning in your cells. Then you may want to pray together about some of the things that have been in the news this week."

An alternative might be for gatherings to meet irregularly, as the need arises. "It would be really helpful to do a short Bible course on one of the gospels." So the congregation reassembles for three sessions, starting with some worship, followed by teaching, and then takes a break till the need to meet arises again.

Might these "not-the-congregations" fill part of the hole being hollowed out by the demise of mid-sized communities? Might they replace po-faced, stuck-in-a-rut worship with more fun, friendly and spontaneous expressions of shared life? Might church regain its licence to thrill?

Church at large

> The Eden Project works with young people on estates in multi-deprived areas of Manchester. Youth cells disciple young people who have responded through the schools work. The young people are also encouraged to attend congregational worship, perhaps in partner churches or with the teams of up to 30 volunteers who live on the estates and model Christian community.
>
> "Planet Life", a monthly youth celebration, and The Tribe's school concerts play a vital role. Both provide an umbilical cord to the wider church. George Lings comments, "A new way of being church has been planted that fits with a world in which younger people relate at the intimate level to members of a peer group but through the media are connected to a much wider world and its cult figures."[10]

Picking and mixing church

A fourth question raised by emerging church concerns the links between fresh expressions and the wider church. Most Christians would take for granted the value of being connected to the whole body of Christ, at least in theory: often the practice is more difficult. Working with other churches in a denomination or through formal ecumenical arrangements can seem life-emptying, dull and bureaucratic – lots of talk for piffling results.

Yet Christians are born into the universal family of God, not

just into a particular expression of church. When the Spirit brings the church home, the end of the journey will be God's global family, stretching back through all history.

St Paul had a vision for making this future a reality in the present. The church in Jerusalem had fallen on financially hard times, so he made strenuous efforts to get his new churches to support the Jerusalem Christians generously. Connecting to the whole meant identifying with weaker parts of the body.

Likewise, fresh expressions of church – and traditional congregations, too! – need to find appropriate ways of being linked to the whole, as they travel with the Spirit to their final destination.

Christian groups can tie into the wider church by attending festivals like Easter People. Through a mission agency they can invite an overseas minister, visiting the country, to lead a series of Bible studies or Holy Week meditations. They can form direct links with a church in another part of the world, with exchange visits if they can afford it.[11]

They can buy CDs, borrow DVDs and visit websites to connect with the Christian community at large. Not far away are affordable large, paper-thin TV screens, possibly hung with pegs. Allied with broadband, they will enable Christian groups to watch a video clip from any part of the planet. A gathering might connect with an overseas partner in real time before launching into prayer: vast potential for tying Christians together around the globe!

Two models

As new expressions of church link with the wider body, what should be the nature of the relationship between emerging and continuing church?

Some argue for a centre-to-the-rim approach. The centre, an existing church, sends out pioneers (to the rim, as it were) to set up new forms of church. These new expressions are linked to the wider church because they were sponsored by the continuing church, and have some loyalty to it.

Churches in a town, for example, might sponsor a teenage congregation, pay for the youth worker, hold the congregation to account and feel some ownership of it. The new congregation in turn, different though it is, feels part of the existing church in the area.

Others believe in a rim-to-the-centre model. Christian entrepreneurs may break away from the inherited church because they feel stifled and in despair. They start to experiment with church, acting independently out on the edge. In due course, they network with other Christians and develop informal links with existing churches "at the centre".[12]

> Forty young people attended a summer "camp" run by Christians. It was a totally new experience, but they loved it. Around 80 have signed up for the following year, a sizable number from an area of social disadvantage. The leaders are praying about a youth worker to help lead the camp. The youth worker would return with the young people from poorer backgrounds, pastor them through the year and help them become an expression of church in their culture. The leaders would pay for the youth worker not through a denomination, but privately.

It may be tempting – though unhelpful – to ask which of these two models is better. Both reflect aspects of the Spirit's work. From-the-centre-to-the-rim perhaps mirrors the outward movement of the Spirit to the world. The-rim-to-the-centre may echo the Spirit's homeward journey, drawing the church toward the Godhead.

Both approaches have been part-and-parcel of church history. The first was reflected in the missionary movement for instance, the second in the origins of many of today's denominations, which began as radical breakaways. Both have played a part in God's purposes.

Sent out in trust

Key issues are trust and accountability. We might say that if mission is at the heart of God and the incarnation was at the heart of God's mission, trust was at the heart of the incarnation. The Father trusted the Son to advance the Kingdom. That pattern has continued. Father and Son exercise trust as they send the Spirit out to the world to advance the Kingdom further.

Jesus trusted his disciples to take his work forward after the ascension. He knew the Spirit would guide them, as part of the Spirit's outward journey. When St Paul had planted a new church, he did not stick around to keep it on the rails. He trusted his appointed leaders to build on what he had started, confident the Spirit would help them. When they loosen tethers and trust pioneers, Christian leaders keep a great tradition alive.

The challenge for the existing church is to create space for people to experiment – and then have faith in them. If pioneers are tied down with endless meetings, getting permission and writing reports, they will either give up or turn their backs on inherited church. They may go it alone. The existing church will be the loser. Trusting pioneers – and encouraging them – is vital if the centre hopes to operate on the rim.

> In 2001 the city-centre clergy fellowship in Belfast established Echo, to engage with the local club culture. Echo runs a fortnightly "godspace" called "God's secret garden" – "A nervous attempt to create Christian community." What does team leader, Dave Magee, most value about his work? "The freedom and trust the clergy have in us. They don't understand the culture and they often don't understand us, but they trust that we are following God and trying to do the right things . . ."[13]

Looking back to be accountable

But if trust is at the heart of the incarnation, accountability is at the heart of trust. It is the other side of the coin. It is hard to exercise trust when the other person does not feel accountable.

Jesus made himself accountable to his Father – "I have come down from heaven not to do my will but to do the will of him who sent me" (John 6:38, NIV). Likewise, the Spirit is not an independent agent. Might there be just the hint of a homeward movement toward the Father and the Son when the Spirit leans toward them, as it were, to listen: "he will not speak on his own authority, but will tell only what he hears" (John 16:13, NEB)?

St Paul, filled with the Spirit, held the leaders of his new churches to account – his letters to Corinth for instance. He also saw himself as accountable to the apostles in Jerusalem, through whom the Spirit made decisions (Acts 15:28). So it is fitting that church pioneers should make themselves accountable as well.

This is especially important in our nerve-jangling society. Non-churchgoers, who worry about so many risks, may have doubts about novel expressions of church. "Can I trust them?" asked a head teacher who had been approached by a Christian to make his school available. "Are they kosher Christian?"

Accountability is a particular challenge to entrepreneurs outside denominations or streams. The mainstream sometimes views them with suspicion. Pioneers are more likely to be accepted by the wider church, as well as by non-believers, if they find suitable ways of being held to account – perhaps through informal links with a respected Christian. A "coaching" model could be particularly effective.

A sense of *mutual* accountability may be important. Can one speak of the three persons of the Trinity being accountable to each other? Certainly, as comes across in 2 Corinthians, Paul had a sense of being accountable to his converts. As pioneers are held to account for their initiatives, perhaps they need to hold the inherited church to account for the adequacy of its support.

"Low control, high accountability" may be an apt description of the Trinity: it is certainly a good motto for emerging church.

Stuart Murray Williams writes:
Mike has put his finger on a key point here. The issue of accountability is crucial for the emerging church – but it

must be relational, liberating and involve mutuality. Old
models of control, risk-aversion and stifling institutional
processes will not do. Most of those involved in emerging
churches long for accountable friendships.

Parts need the whole

Some in emerging church circles are so disenchanted with
church that they want to turn their back on it. With rare abandon they do away with sermons, scrap teaching, dispense with
leaders ("it's community that counts"), do worship their way
and go straight to Scripture, "googling" for truth through
discussions that are unencumbered by tradition. They don't
want to be boxed in.

This bracing radicalism risks throwing out the accumulated
wisdom of the church with the bathwater. New Testament
churches had lots of autonomy, but they did not free-wheel over
the core teaching of the faith. The apostles took care to pass on
the basic tenets of Christian belief accurately (eg 1 Corinthians
15:3). Local churches were instructed, rebuked and encouraged
through letters from acknowledged leaders of the wider church.
From the earliest days, there was a universal component to
church.

To be authentic, tailor-made church will seek a path between
anarchic bottom-up and straitjacketed top-down approaches to
truth. Jesus did not impose hard-and-fast propositions on
people, nor did he preach anything-goes laissez-faire. He used
parables to invite individuals to explore his teaching. His stories
had fuzzy edges, leaving room for further questions.

Emerging churches may need to follow Jesus in combining a
corpus of truth with permission to explore. They will access the
insights of the wider church, but allow individuals to chart their
way through received teaching at different paces, with varied
emphases and with a diversity of application. Truth will become
a family album with many pages.

For example, some gatherings are replacing sermons with
group Bible study. This can be great for participation, learning

and strengthening community, but it risks letting the blind lead the blind. So why not ring the changes – use a teaching video occasionally, make Bible study aids available to groups as they study, or encourage someone to listen perhaps to a relevant sermon tape, obtained from another church or a conference, and resource the discussion.

Worship options will proliferate, too, as technology leaps ahead. No need to use a band these days, you can use a CD. Forget being stuck in one tradition, you can plunder them all. Looking for some material? Go on to the Net. Gone are the days when the universal body of Christ equalled standardised church: now and in future it will support more customised expressions. The capsule of the inherited church is being shattered. Christian communities are free to explore.

Goodbye place?

In the 1960s Dr Beeching caused uproar when he proposed closing hundreds of railway lines in Britain. Some fear that emerging church represents an "ecclesiastical Beeching"[14] – a movement that will lead to a wholesale withdrawal from much-loved, and often very beautiful church buildings. As one lay leader in the Church of England asked me, "What will happen to the buildings? That is the bottom line, isn't it?"

Pioneers of emerging church, with their emphasis on community, would answer with an emphatic "No!" Some think that we can't shed church buildings fast enough. Others would add that a fixation with buildings reinforces a "come" rather than "go" approach to mission.

Skip church and pray in a café?

Yet it would be easy to turn away from buildings too sharply. For groups not gathering in people's homes, finding somewhere to meet, getting access when they want and setting up the room week after week can be a real chore. Ask any church plant that has been doing it for several years!

Buildings can also give a tangible sense of identity. Several cells may want to be part of a larger whole, but if there is no building to symbolise that community, individuals may find it harder to belong.

"Sacred space" is important for many worshippers – a place that is set apart for prayer, that feels special, that may have a spiritual ambience. Church buildings can have that quality, not least because they have been prayed in for years.

Quite a few emerging churches use traditional buildings because they are practical, the building strengthens their identity or they value a sense of the Spirit's presence. But church buildings do not suit everyone – hence Christian groups in cafés, pubs, schools or at home.

The first Christians did not meet in church buildings, but the later ones did. So there is no rule here. Perhaps the key issue is intentionality: "Is God calling us as a group to think about space? What might we do to help this space express the presence of God? Given that the Spirit dwells in the physical world, can we create a context that is welcoming to the Spirit?"

Humans are of course physical beings and affected by their physical environment. They can be stressed by it – endless noise and traffic for example, and they can be restored by it – a walk in the countryside. So inevitably the physical setting will influence how Christians relate together and worship. Can emerging church create something of "the beauty of holiness" wherever it meets?

Geography's coming home

The mantra is that geographical communities are giving way to networks of interest. People do not relate to others in the same place, but to individuals with the same interests from much further afield. Emerging church responds to this trend by seeking to be church for specific networks rather than particular places.

The reality is more complex. As we saw in Chapter Three, for many people the local context is very alive. They put down roots, slowly get to know their neighbours and may welcome a local, "root" expression of church. Others, who may attend a network church, will have some aspect of place in common – the same city, town, suburb or county. Place will not be what brings them together, but it will be in the background, an additional strand binding the group.

Symbols of place – the local newspaper, local radio, the pub, a well-travelled street or the supermarket – provide a sense of belonging. They create a "symbolic community". Individuals identify with the symbols of a place, and what happens to these symbols matters to them.

Is God calling leaders of emerging (as well as continuing) church to take place seriously, as part of Christian discipleship? Mounting interest in creation theology, not least in some emerging church circles, may point in this direction. Caring for your physical locality brings "the environment" home.

It may also strengthen community, another value within some new expressions of church. Bothering only with your network may limit your horizons to people you associate with. But if you value your neighbourhood, you will be more likely to care for an older person down the street or a physically disabled person on the corner. Extending care to people who might be neglected brings community to their front door.

Better communications mean that what is "local" has broadened out. Local for one person may be their neighbourhood, for someone else their town and for someone else their county or region. Some people will have overlapping notions of what is local. This may create opportunities for emerging church to serve a mixture of neighbourhood, town-wide and regional needs in a way that the very-local church could not. Might emerging church, a minister asked, be an opportunity for the church to be more serious about regionality?

The Spirit loves the physical

All this means that there is no need to substitute "place rules" – meet in traditional buildings and serve the streets nearby –

with another set of tramlines: scrap buildings and forget geography. There is cathedral room for flexibility. Some fresh expressions of church may value traditional buildings: others may create "sacred space" in secular contexts. Some may serve people in a specific neighbourhood: others may reach a network far and wide.

What's important is that emerging church travels with the Spirit. The Spirit's outward movement to the world is not just to people, but to the physical environment as well. The Spirit indwells the whole of creation to sustain it. Fresh expressions of church will be led by the Spirit when they, too, go out to creation to embrace and love it. The building in which Christians meet (of whatever kind) is a good place to begin. So is the local area, however defined.

Equally, the Spirit's homeward movement draws not only the church toward the Godhead, but the entire creation. The physical world will be made new when the Spirit's journey is complete. Fresh, as well as traditional expressions of church, travel with the Spirit when they seek to improve the environment and mend broken communities. Again, the local is a good place to start. Far from being against place, emerging church should be its champion – in a dazzling display of versatility.

Farewell to old names?

Emerging church turns over the soil in one further part of the garden: can we abandon terms like congregation and church?

We have been using the word "church" with rare abandon. But some in emerging church would like to drop the term. They work with people for whom the word is a strong put-off. It has connotations of hierarchy, being out of date, formality and being cold! It reminds some people of unhappy encounters with the church.

Others would also like to abandon the word "congregation". It conjures up ideas of a fixed group of people, meeting at a fixed time, in a fixed place, with a fixed way of doing things. It represents all that they are trying to get away from. It cuts across their attempt to be church, but "not the church".

In our fluid culture, it is tempting to be fluid with language. Probably not much is at stake with the word "congregation": if the cap doesn't fit, why wear it? But more may be at risk with "church". The term has been used so widely for so many centuries that it has an iconic status. It helps to define Christian identity – "I'm part of the visible body of Christ, called church."

Completely rejecting the word "church" would be highly symbolic. It could undermine the notion that existing and emerging churches are interdependent – that despite their differences they are part of the same body. Dropping the term "church" might be misunderstood as a more total rejection of continuing church than was intended – not quite a slap in the face, but something like it.

In Michael Riddell's phrase, some experimenters with church may want to be "bilingual". They might drop "church" when relating to individuals in their mission context, as part of the Spirit's outward journey, but use it in their dialogue with the inherited church, as they accompany the Spirit home.

Sometimes the term "church" is positively helpful. If a group of teenagers is functioning as a church, avoiding the label may be to shoot oneself in the foot. The young people may thoroughly enjoy their group, but never think of it as a church. Church, for them, may be that "boring stuff" on Sunday. When they become young adults, they may be less inclined to join the church because of its negative connotations. It may never cross their minds that church can be fun. Language makes a difference.

Rethinking church

Fresh expressions of church raise all sorts of questions about what we mean by church – what really defines church? How important is it for Christians to meet physically together? Should we be content with tiny, dispersed groups of Christians, or should we aim to draw these groups together into larger gatherings – of what size?

As emerging church connects with the wider church, how can we foster accountability and trust, and use the whole to encourage individual parts to explore? What is the role of place – buildings and locality – in the mission of emerging church? Do we need to "mind our language" – dropping the word "congregation" where appropriate, but keeping "church"? Pioneers may have to ask these questions as fresh expressions of church mature.

More important, if you really can't get out of a problem by using the same kind of thinking that got you into the problem, re-imagining church could not be more urgent. The questions posed by emerging church are an essential first step. They point to some very different, creative ways of being a Christian community.

These alternatives may bring shock and awe to Christians with an inherited mindset. But working through the issues could help at least some churchgoers to abandon rigid patterns of thought and be open to new ideas. Throwing off preconceptions would be a giant leap toward fresh expressions of church.

So there is no need to be stuck with a hand-me-down version of church. The very shape of church is up for grabs.

Notes

1. An example, though some of his views are controversial, is Paul S. Fiddes, *Participating in God*, London: DLT, 2000.
2. I am grateful to the New Testament scholar, Dr Alan Garrow, for pointing this out to me, based on his interpretation of Didache 9 and Didache 10, two sections of a first-century document that throws light on early Christian communities.
3. George Lings, "Joining the club – or changing the rules?", *Encounters on the Edge*, No. 5, Church Army: The Sheffield Centre, pp. 10–15.

4. *Mission-shaped Church*, London: Church House Publishing, 2004, p. 99.
5. www.emergingchurch.info.
6. Pete Ward, *Liquid Church*, Carlisle: Paternoster, 2002, esp. Chapter Four.
7. Robert Wuthnow, *Sharing the Journey. Support Groups and America's New Quest for Community*, New York: The Free Press, 1996, pp. 343–47.
8. *Ibid.*, pp. 355–60.
9. Cautioning against abandoning the congregational model of church, Stuart Murray comments, "Asking radical questions does not always result in the rejection of tried and tested answers." Stuart Murray, *Church Planting. Laying Foundations*, Carlisle: Paternoster, 1998, p. 230.
10. George Lings, "The Eden Puzzle", *Encounters on the Edge*, No. 14, Church Army: The Sheffield Centre, 2002, p. 20.
11. *Connect* is a collaborative venture by various mission agencies to encourage churches to link with churches overseas and become globally connected.
12. Some in emerging church circles would reject the notion of a centre and a rim altogether. Taking their cue from postmodern philosophy, they would claim that there is no centre and rim, only interlocking circles. Effectively, from one point of view, they are operating on a rim-to-the-centre basis, but they would not see it in those terms – "one person's network is another's periphery".
13. www.emergingchurch.info/stories/café/davemagee.
14. Nick Spencer, *Parochial Vision*, Carlisle: Paternoster, 2004, p. xiii.

CHAPTER SEVEN

DOWN TO THE LOCAL

She was full of enthusiasm. "Thank you for what you said. I have just taken over our 'Mums-and-tots' group. Most of its members don't come to church. I have been praying that God will give me a vision for the group. I think I now know what to do. I'm going to see if it can become a congregation." A while later I asked the minister what happened. "It was a disaster. She rushed in with the *Alpha* course. Some people were enthused. But it blew the group apart" – operation partly successful, patient dead.

Emerging church is no easy gig: it is full of pitfalls. "Blowing the group apart" is just one. George Lings and Stuart Murray Williams, reviewing church planting in the 1990s, mention others: cloning not creating, failing to let the context shape church and the mismatch of resources to task. They report:

Conversations revealed demanding dynamics for which planting teams did not adequately allow:

- the pressure of keeping motivation alive;
- the attrition of weekly setting-up;
- ceaseless creativity in worship;
- a constant multifaceted learning curve;
- a widening agenda as the church matured;

- a misunderstanding by surrounding churches.

These factors were especially onerous where leadership was part-time or voluntary and church life was not kept simple.'[1]

New expressions of church are not a quick fix, a panacea to halt church decline. They require careful thought and planning. Clearly prayer, authentic witness to the gospel and openness to the Spirit will have to be at the epicentre of any fresh expression. But what else would be involved?

In this chapter we look at some issues that individual congregations might want to consider in starting a new form of church, and in the next what action denominations and streams could take. These chapters are not a template. Emerging church is about jumping out of pre-ordained models, not being tied down by a new "right way". Yet some people want a concrete picture of how emerging church might pan out. They want to "see" it before they buy into it. Thinking through what might be entailed can help to paint that picture.

Churches walking down experiment street might ask of a proposed venture:

Who's it from?
Who's it by?
Who's it with?
What will go on?
How will it move on?
Why will it keep on?[2]

Who's it from?

A new expression of church may be a "lone ranger", independent of any denomination or network: some pioneers have their salaries paid by friends. Or it may be kicked off by a denomination or "stream". Or it may be the child of a mission agency. Spurgeon's College and Oasis Trust, for example, launched

Urban Expression, which places teams of church planters in under-churched areas of east London.

Owning the vision

For an individual church, "Who's it from?" may be a question about who owns the vision within the parent church. And that of course will depend on how the vision was arrived at, and perhaps also its content.

What might be the vision? In today's splintering society, visions for emerging church are bound to vary. They will have different values and goals. Yet although "mimic the model" should be an anathema, some values – those discussed in Chapter Two perhaps – should jump the differences. Sound values will provide a genetically healthy start.

> One group of church leaders asked themselves whether they should have a three-part set of values: a short statement making clear that any fresh expression must be based on Scripture and the historic creeds of the church; a longer statement of core values; and a third section setting out some first steps and long-term hopes for the venture. This third part would need to be revised in the light of experience.

Obviously a vision for emerging church needs some blessing from the existing church. This will be important if staff time and money are to be spent on the initiative. It will help the new venture to be recognised as a valid expression of church – vital if new and old are to see themselves as interdependent and do some things together. It may also avoid difficulties further down the line.

As it matures, the fledgling congregation could have a significant impact on the parent who gave birth to it. It may change how the budget is allocated, who is in leadership, how the church defines its mission – and even the parent's identity. These changes will be easier to negotiate if members fully owned the vision at the beginning.

The staff of a largish church in west London wanted to explore emerging church. They spent half a day with an outside consultant, who had had some experience of this. They discussed the mindset required, and brainstormed some possibilities. After the consultant had left, they reviewed the session and decided to involve the wider leadership.

They invited the consultant to spend a day with their church council nine months later. Again, the session started with the emerging church mindset. There was input on "questions to think about" if the church decided to go down this path. The council then brainstormed the opportunities and problems.

At the end of the day, the council passed a resolution. It welcomed their minister's intention to spend a sabbatical examining fresh expressions of church. It asked their minister to work with a small group of lay people to make arrangements for the whole church to learn about emerging church. (One possibility was to have a church weekend away, devoted to this.) And it affirmed the principle that any new expression of church should "travel light" – it should be simple, realistic and easy on people's time.

A small step can be a big leap

Getting a permission slip from church members may not be easy. They may find it hard to accept that newcomers will not graduate to the "main" congregation. They may struggle to see a very different style of worship as "proper" church. They may fear being neglected, especially if the minister spends time on the new venture. And they may feel undervalued: all the buzz is about something new – "are we being left behind?"

The ideal, of course, is that members don't expect their old vision to be the new vision, that they do embrace a fresh expression of church. But what happens if you've got a congregation that clings crab-like to the inside of its shell, only occasionally letting a claw out to check that the world is safe? What might you do then?

Starting small might be the answer. Perhaps a minister finds one or two church members willing to build a cell of enthusiastic Christians, with a mission group in mind. The cell meets regularly to pray and plan. It launches some activities for non-churchgoers, such as a pub quiz, a divorce recovery group or a reading group. The elders are informed and asked to give it their blessing.

As friendships develop, non-churchgoers may be invited to a *Y-course* (for people with no church background), next *Christianity Explored* (or the equivalent) and then a discipleship series. In time, they become a Christian cell, meeting separately from the original group, which has continued its regular meetings. One cell has become two

Some members of the new cell might be invited to meet with the elders, share their stories, explain why the parent church is not for them and describe their vision for the future. Personal testimony is very compelling. In the light of what they have heard, the elders might invite the original cell leader to convene a cluster – the two cells together.

The cells might continue to meet separately, but sometimes cluster in an informal, relaxed meeting, perhaps over a meal. In threes and fours participants might share what God was doing in their lives, videos, audio tapes and new media might provide some input, and the cluster might discuss ways of growing a third cell.

All this takes time. At each critical stage the elders are asked for support. They are not invited to endorse a whole new development in advance – the initiative might not even evolve as originally expected. Their support comes in bite-sized chunks. The continuing church learns what God is doing through experience.

This approach would not be without risks. What would happen if down the track the new expression of church became increasingly novel, and the elders wanted to dump it? Clearly, it would be safer to get support at the beginning for the basic principles. But where this is impossible, a compromise step-by-step approach may be an alternative.

One minister asked, "Why not adopt both approaches at the same time? You might encourage the congregation to welcome the principles of emerging church. Simultaneously, the minister might launch a prototype, to gain experience and provide an example."

Who's it by?

All the experience of church leadership, indeed leadership in any walk of life, is that teams are vital. They provide leaders with support and mix up complementary skills. New expressions of church vary, and so inevitably the teams leading them will differ too. People planning to "do" emerging church may want to ask these sorts of questions.

Who will lead the team?

Some ministers may be the most natural choice because they have pastoral contacts, they have the expertise, they would relish the challenge and they have the time. But others will have clogged-up lives. It does not take long for clergy diaries to reach breaking point, nor for church members to impose their expectations on what ministers should do. Changing tack after being in post for a while is not easy.

For clergy so fortunate, a sabbatical may be the chance to refocus their ministry. The church will survive without them for several months. Perhaps those who pick up some of the minister's tasks can be persuaded to keep them on, releasing the minister for a new venture.

Other clergy may feel ill-equipped to lead a new expression of church. They may feel called to pastoral ministry rather than mission, or may struggle to imagine a new form of church. Still others may think they know "the right way" to do church and be reluctant to abandon the model. .

Even so, hesitant clergy can play a key role, so long as they put aside some of their preconceptions of church. They can encourage lay people to take the initiative, support and oversee them, interface between them and others in the church and perhaps offer some input.

Alternatively, if finances allow, a church might pay a member of staff to be a full-time catalyst for fresh expressions. St Mary's Upton, an Anglican church in the Wirral, has appointed an Associate Vicar specifically to encourage new forms of church.

> **Stuart Murray Williams writes:**
> *How much involvement in emerging churches dare we allow clergy to have? Sure, they have theological training, leadership experience and institutional authentication. But what else do they bring with them? What will they infect emerging churches with? In any case, maybe emerging churches are casting doubt on the whole clergy–laity divide. Certainly leadership values, models and tasks are very different in some emerging churches.*

How big a team?

It used to be said that church plants required as many people as possible. Critical mass would provide the breakthrough.

But that story was turned on its stamen when large middle-class teams proved to be a cultural invasion among the urban poor. Articulate middle-class arrivals cramped the expression of local gifts. Elsewhere, "critical mass" meant that the planting group set the agenda. Members worshipped as *they* wanted, which drew in their Christian friends but did little to attract non-churchgoers. "Beware Christians! They'll wreck it!" seemed only a slight exaggeration. Small teams seemed the answer.

Just as this new orthodoxy was gaining ground, Manchester's Eden Project burst on the scene. On each estate where it is present, the Project has teams of three or four paid school workers, supported by up to 30 volunteers. These volunteers come from a variety of backgrounds, but they are committed to the area and live there – more like immigrants than commuters. In effect, the Eden Project offers community-based mission, built around a sizable Christian group. This seems highly appropriate for work among disaffected young people, where resources are scarce.[3]

The moral? Emerging church has values, but not rules. The size of the team will depend on the task and the circumstances.

What skills and expertise?

Chapter Four mentioned initiating, networking, facilitating and resource-gathering as perhaps the minimum skills required to lead enquirers into a new way of church. Expertise in some form of community or "consumer" service may also be required, as we shall see. Several of these skills may be combined in one person.

" 'See how these Christians love each other' was not just a passing compliment, it was the single largest missionary dynamic of the early church."[4] If George Lings's comment is true, then someone who is a great lover of people and knowledgeable about team-building will be crucial, perhaps the person with facilitation skills.

Team members with the right mindset will be vital. Their aim will not be to create echo-church, but an expression of church that fits the context. Viewing church through the same lens will be essential.

Where can we get the resources?

This is often the first base – no resources, no action. Some churches shrink from new ideas because they think they could never do it. Yet people with the will and the skills may exist in a church, if they are asked. Remember the woman and the sewing circle in Chapter Four?

Or neighbouring churches may be able to pool resources. In the emerging world of "personalised scale", organisations are forging alliances to customise their offerings. Different products may be wound together, for example, to produce a package tailored to a specific group. The same principle applies to church: churches may have to cooperate to be culturally specific. Many teenage and youth congregations have emerged on a collaborative basis.

Alternatively, help may be at hand from elsewhere – government funding in some cases, or support from a mission agency, such as the Church of England's Church Army. As the plight of the church in the West becomes increasingly dire, will more and more mission agencies find that requests to support emerging church hit the top of their in-trays?

What training and support does the team need?

Though training and other resources are becoming available, they remain limited because emerging church is so young. This will change as emerging church climbs the agenda. In the meantime, the best way to learn about new forms of church may be to speak to others doing it. The Appendix suggests some ports of call.

Could emerging church take a leaf from the secular world? As we hurtle into the future, learning networks will transform the workplace. Even now, some chief executives give up half a day a month to meet with peers from non-competing organisations. They bring a business problem and seek advice. It is highly effective, they find support in what can be a lonely job and it's cheaper than management consultants! There may be lessons here for pioneers of emerging church.[5]

In addition of course, the team will need support from the church's leaders and a means of being held to account. Accountability based on a framework of values is often recommended. Individuals and groups can be given extensive freedom, so long as they keep within the spirit of the agreed values.

Who's it with?

Leaders of "nouvelle" church may want to ask, "Who do we plan to work with?"

- *Existing members who are disillusioned and about to leave?* This would be worthwhile, but has the danger that the new expression of church will be designed with just existing churchgoers in mind. Could disillusioned members be enthused by the idea of developing a form of church that appeals to their non-churchgoing friends, or that serves a socially excluded group nearby?

- *People who come to fringe activities but are not engaged with regular church?* This would require careful discussion with the leaders of the groups involved. What are the expectations of those who take part? Would any of them value a more explicit spiritual dimension? How might this be made available without putting pressure on people?

- *People beyond the fringe, in the wider community?* A number of them will have had some experience of church, others won't. It will help to be clear about which group you plan to engage with. If a team aims to serve people with no church background, obviously it will need to start much "further back" in introducing them to the gospel. Most likely it will be in for a long, though exciting journey. Has the team got the stamina?

Building on what you're doing

To help answer "Who's it with?" it may be worth asking, "Who are we best connected with?" "What resources do we have that we can share with people outside church?" "What are we doing now that we can build on?"

> One minister asked advice about starting emerging church. When I asked, "What are you doing already?" she described an older people's luncheon club that had recently opened. It had swelled to about 30 and seemed set for further growth. "Would they welcome a spiritual element in their meetings?" If so, could she envisage stepping-stones to a fuller expression of church? She became thoughtful. What she had imagined would be a radically new venture now seemed, instead, to be an extension of what was already in place.

Many churches have a strong presence in the community, "beyond the fringe". Some have a big involvement in schools, and may even appoint schools' workers. These activities could be a place to start. Might schools be the mission opportunity of the century?

> Mark Griffiths, for example, has long experience of running after-school clubs for primary-age children. Attached to St Mary's Milton Keynes, he now runs a Saturday morning club for 120 children, the great majority of whom are strangers to church. He first built relationships with the local schools. Then he advertised "We'll do life application lessons and Bible stories", so that the Christian content was upfront.
>
> A typical session starts with 45 minutes of play, children choosing from a range of activities. The next 45 minutes involves all ages (5 to 11) together, with ice-breaker games and group activities. The final 30 minutes comprise Bible-based teaching, based on stories. There is constant background music for the first 90 minutes. But when the stories begin, the music stops. That changes the atmosphere and helps the children to quieten down.[6] The children love it.
>
> Parents pay £1 a session for each child. They get a much-needed breathing space, the children are cared for and, although "it's not for me", parents hope the Christian input will do the children some good. The club is a service to parents, as much as to children.
>
> What happens when the children become too old for the club? In his previous after-school clubs, Mark had tried to integrate the children with church-based youth work, but it had not really worked. The cultures were too different. We discussed whether he should encourage the children to stay together and form, in effect, a young teenagers' congregation. Why not a children's congregation, a young teens' congregation and eventually a youth congregation for older teenagers?

Be specific!

Some in emerging church circles are eager to reach everyone. "After all," they say, "God has opened himself to all-comers. Shouldn't we do the same?"

But this faces a practical hurdle. It is impossible to reach everyone at the same time. To serve non-believers the church has to be culturally sensitive. Teenagers have different interests to parents, single mothers have a different focus to a single girl.

Trying to embrace everyone, week in and week out, would be an extraordinary task. "Non-Christians should not have to endure cultural circumcision when they go to church."[7]

Complete openness would also have to leap a theological fence. Just as Jesus became human in a specific culture, so the Spirit is immersed in different cultures. Diversity is one of the "faces of God" reflected in emerging church.

So in asking "Who's it with?", a planning group may want to start with wide horizons. But gradually it will need to home in on a specific group: "these are the particular people we want to serve at this stage." Finding the right niche is critical.

What will go on?

This is a question about the nature of the new venture – what will go on within it? The church in Ukraine has a stunning answer. It intends to plant 28,000 churches by the year 2015. It is up to 6,000 already. The strategy? Find ways of meeting human needs in the cities church plans to reach. Before grace is preached, it is first practised.[8]

Coming near you: a church that cares?

Worship first doesn't work. That's what "Stepping Stones" discovered. Stepping Stones is a fresh expression of church on a tough housing estate in South Anston, a large village to the east of Sheffield. At one stage 40% of properties were boarded up.

Stepping Stones began as a church plant meeting in the church hall. But it was an uphill struggle from day one, and the plant nearly died. The turning point came with the appointment of two Church Army officers, Paul and Sheelagh Easby. They continued the Sunday services, but also started an after-school "Kids Klub", then "Girl Thing" (a "kids klub" for secondary school children), next parenting groups and eventually Kabblestones, a Tuesday afternoon cell meeting for older people.

None of these activities were large, but they were sustainable and helped Stepping Stones to become an accepted part of the community landscape. In place of "quick fix" evangelism, community

> activities have become steps toward a dispersed community of God throughout the estate. Though the struggle remains tortuous at times, Stepping Stones is increasingly independent of its parent.[9]

Sometimes people think that the essence of a church plant is worship. Start a new "worship centre", perhaps in a different style, and non-churchgoers will come. That may have worked in the past (sometimes). It may also be appropriate for disenchanted church members, for whom worship feels stale and irrelevant.

But as the chasm opens up between church and contemporary culture, worship-first will be a strategy of the past. Growing numbers of people are uninterested in Christianity. Invite them to an event where Christian belief is explained, and they will politely say "No thanks".

If they do attend, unless they know them well, their relationship to the organisers will be akin to that between an advertiser and a consumer: organisers are trying to "sell" the faith. Church may think it is an act of love to tell people about the gospel, but many on the other end – jaundiced by marketing – will not see it in that way. They won't say to themselves "I'm being loved", they will think "I'm being sold something".

A senior strategist in a large advertising agency described how "consumers are no longer loyal to brands, brands are having to learn how to be loyal to consumers". This shift affects church. Before preaching the gospel, the church has to prove that it is loyal to the people it wants to reach.

The Acts of the Apostles links the early church's growth to the way the first Christians enjoyed the favour of all the people (Acts 5:12–14). Initiators of emerging church might ask, "What would we have to do to win the favour of the people round us?" The answer of course is "to love them to bits".

What might that actually mean? Following best mission practice, it will almost certainly involve some form of service. Time and again Jesus did not start by proclaiming the gospel, but with acts of service – healing and other forms of kindness.

Individuals were not potential recruits to the cause: they were people with a variety of needs.

Meeting the real needs of people – "consumer" needs such as having fun, and "community" needs such as supporting single parents in looking after their children – will increasingly be the kernel of new expressions of church.

> This is the approach of the Revd Penny Joyce, on the brand new Madley House housing estate, Witney in Oxfordshire. She tried an *Alpha* course, leafleted the 300 houses on the estate, but it didn't work. So now she is concentrating on "Discovery Days".
>
> On a Wednesday in the back room of a new school, a mums-and-tots group makes way for a luncheon club, which in turn makes way for a very lively after-school club. So many children are in the after-school club, it has split into two sessions. A book group is about to start, and discussion evenings.
>
> "We need to build community first, and out of that community create church," she said. "Building community is what is happening here and now." Serving other people – that skipped sentence in some forms of evangelism – is at the heart of her approach.[10]

Mission-shaped church is not about well-intentioned "grab and run" forays into the surrounding culture: it is about putting down deep roots of love among people who do not attend church. It is about acts of kindness that are not just the d'hors d'oevres of church, but are a meal in their own right. It is about service before services.

"Brailling" the culture

"Brailling" means feeling, touching and sensing the world around you – reading your community.[11] It is mission by engagement. Any church wanting to serve its network or neighbourhood will first need to listen carefully. Andrew Hamilton, in Brighton, Australia reflected recently:

Our "church planting" adventure has entered a new phase with our family this week moving into the community we are going to be part of . . . As I began to reflect on this idea of programs as "bridges to the community" I got disturbed. I mean, have we ever really thought through what that says?

It seems to me, to imply that there is the church community and then there is the local community, and these are two separated entities. And because of that we need to try and connect them – because typically they are not well connected. Somehow we need to create ways for church folks to mix it up with those who are not part of our churches . . .

Programs that serve the community are great, but I am not convinced that people who have either intentionally or unintentionally isolated themselves from "the world" will make genuine connections in any program . . . for now I will be burning my bridges.[12]

To read people you have to live with them. Is that an overstatement? Certainly churchgoers must be involved in the everyday lives of people if they want to serve them. They will become aware of unmet needs and possibilities for action.

Of course, a church may be overwhelmed by the number of opportunities, by the different ways of meeting any one need or by uncertainty about what can be done with scarce resources. It may need to keep listening to the community and "waiting on God" till the way forward becomes clear. This is a process of "double listening" – listening to the culture, and listening to God through Scripture and the insights of believers.

Listening to the community can occur through personal friendships, involvement in community events and more formal methods, such as a survey or audit.[13] One church is considering the use of focus groups: "Let's invite some of our non-church-going neighbours to meet over a few months and advise on what we should do with this new building. At each stage, we can test the options on them."

Another group of Christians came together from different churches to explore an "action-reflection" way of doing theology. They started by sharing their stories, often of struggle. From this sharing grew a sense of what was lacking in the neighbourhood. Few facilities were available for people to meet socially, and there was little sense of community.

The group decided to do some research. They visited hundreds of homes, and interviewed dozens of local groups and services. They discovered that what people wanted was a neighbourhood centre.

But they did not act on this immediately. Instead, they "went to the Bible" to prepare themselves for the journey ahead. They became aware that struggle is a constant theme in Scripture. They might have missed this if they hadn't looked at the Bible through the prism of their own personal struggles and the task ahead of them.

The reassurance that God was with them in the midst of struggle was to prove vital as they began to consider what they could actually do. Eventually, they adapted their own church building to make it available to the community.

The group had begun with their own experiences, then listened to the experiences of their neighbourhood, next they had turned to Scripture, and finally in the light of this "double listening" they started to act – experience, reflection, action.[14]

Researching the options will help to prevent "eyes wide shut" to the opportunities for service. It will focus prayer, avoid mistakes and help the church tune in to the culture it seeks to reach. Members will imbibe bottom-up ways of being church, and contacts with non-churchgoers will be strengthened. Above all, it will be an act of love. In Bishop John Saxbee's phrase, church can only go and tell when it has first been and listened.

Do someone a favour

What might result from listening? Many churches run a variety of community programmes from toy groups, to bereavement call-in centres, to ecology groups, to parenting classes, to self-help groups, to keep-fit classes, to film clubs, to debt counselling, to healthy-living clubs, to painters' workshops, to book clubs, to skittle evenings, to AIDS awareness groups and countless others.

It used to be thought that people first believed the gospel, then decided to belong to church and then changed their behaviour. That has been replaced by the new mantra, "belonging before believing". People first experience Christian community. Having belonged, they believe and then change their behaviour.

May there be occasions when we need to change the mantra again? Increasingly, the church may want to engage non-believers first at the point of behaviour, helping them with behaviours that are a problem such as addiction, stress, marital breakdown, parenting or handling conflict at work.

As implicit Christian values are brought to bear on these problems, individuals may start to behave in a Kingdom way long before they sign up to the gospel. Gradually, they may be drawn into a more explicit form of Christian community and then into faith – behaviour, belonging, believing; a reversal of the original model.

This opens the possibility that discipleship may start well before individuals have "signed on the dotted line". Participants may learn Christian principles of parenting, money management or safe sex before they assent to Christian belief. They may have quite a full experience of church before knowing that it is church.

How will it move on?

It is one thing to provide some form of community or consumer service to people, quite another to use this as a starting point to explore the gospel. Many people can see how a church might serve its community, or how it might do evangelism. "But how do you bring the two together? How do you invite participants in a community or consumer activity to move on? If people join a group on one agenda, how do you introduce them to a totally different, spiritual agenda?"

If emerging church can answer that question, might it help to heal the schism that sometimes exists between proclaiming the gospel and social action?

Please, no catches!

"I went on *Alpha,*" a colleague confessed, "but they didn't get me!" Manipulation is a danger in any kind of evangelism. It is a special risk if you hope participants in a community or leisure activity, such as a social club, will explore Christian belief. Adding a spiritual dimension to such a group will need careful thought – "Is that what members signed up for?"

More than anything, mission is about love, not raking in converts. So valuing the group for what it is now is vital: it is a form of unconditional love. This is a love which says, "Even if you show not the slightest interest in the Christian faith, I'm glad to be with you, I shall cherish the best in you and I shall thank God for you. Respecting God's gift to you of choice matters more than whether or not you choose to examine Christian belief."

Paradoxically, loving people like that will encourage them to trust you. So the more relaxed you feel about where people are on their spiritual journeys, the more ready they may be to travel with you the next mile.

Adding spiritual value from the start

Some fresh expressions of church start with an explicitly Christian element from day one. Service and proclamation join up straight away. The children's Saturday club led by Mark Griffiths would be an example.

Being up-front about the spiritual dimension is obviously important. It needs to be clear in the publicity and perhaps reinforced at the first meeting. Someone hosting "spiritual cinema" for example might say, "The aim of these evenings is to have a good time, watch an interesting film, and discuss some of the moral and spiritual questions that the film raises. Our 'golden rule' is to respect the right of people to disagree. I come from a Christian background, so that will clearly influence my contribution. It also affects my hopes for the group – that we might be able to support one another and experiment with some

expressions of spirituality. But obviously that will be up to the group. I'd like to suggest, though, that we have a time of still-ness at the end of each meeting, when we can get in touch with God as we understand him (or her), reflect on the evening or become at peace with our inner selves. What do you think?"

In time, those periods of quietness might become a bridge-head into a further examination of spirituality. Perhaps the group started by meeting every month, and then members decide to add an "in-between" meeting to discuss what spirit-uality might mean in everyday life.

> In a very different example, a Yorkshire group of Christians began a monthly "seeker" service in a pub, with an attractive presentation on a Christian theme. They started by inviting their non-believing friends. Gradually the word spread and after two years a significant number were coming. The presentations tapped into a longing for significance. A network emerged that enjoyed these presentations as a form of entertainment and a source of friendship.
>
> The next step was an invitation to a short series exploring basic Christianity. Around 10 or so came. After the course, they were invited to form what was effectively a discipleship group. The group now meets weekly, with a different topic each time, and has grown to around 20. It has experimented with different forms of worship – listening to reflective music and singing songs. But after a year, members were still trying to discover what form of worship would work best for them.
>
> Meanwhile, the monthly seeker events have continued. The next step will be to hold another Christian discovery course, and to invite the graduates of that course to join the discipleship group. It is hoped that a discovery course every year might be realistic, and that in two or three years it may be possible to launch a second discipleship group. These groups, the leader hopes, will eventually become small congregations.

Adding spiritual value later

Sometimes a spiritual dimension grows spontaneously, after a group has met for a while.

> In one area of social disadvantage, some of the more renowned teenagers got to know the new assistant minister. They started gathering in the back of the church on Thursday evenings. There was no great plan, the group just evolved. The young people quizzed the minister about God, and God became a regular topic of conversation. After a while, the young people let slip that they loved the music from *Sister Act*. Could they sing some of the songs? So the minister got hold of the music and encouraged them to sing and dance to it. Might this become a step into worship and the very beginnings of church?

Many initiatives take a different tack. They start with some form of consumer or community service, from social events to social action. Then, having developed networks of trust, individuals are invited to a further group, in which Christianity is explored. The explicitly Christian element is kept separate from the original group.

Some youth churches are exploring this model. Churchgoers may think a youth congregation is culturally hip simply because it exists, but to many young people it can seem as culturally becalmed as traditional church.

One approach – to connect with the culture – is to help young people acquire a qualification, or a dance group to prepare for a performance, or to offer courses for young people wanting to make a CD or film. From each group or course a cell might form for those who want to explore health or other issues. The hope is that the cell will be a setting in which to raise spiritual questions. Perhaps it will gradually evolve into an expression of church.

Whether the context is younger or older people, individuals can be encouraged to join the new cell if the idea is introduced gradually. As one senior businessman remarked, "It's much easier to get people to accept a big change a year away than a small one in a week's time."

Sometimes the way can be prepared in the very first meeting of the larger group. The leader might say, "We're here for a six week course on stress management. I hope that we shall all enjoy it and learn from each other. At the end of the course, I shall offer some voluntary sessions on spiritual resources that can help us put into practice what we have learnt."

The leader might mention the "after course" in a low key way at each of the six sessions – "If you're wondering whether you can ever do this stuff, you may like to come to the sessions on spiritual resources, if we decide we want them."

As time goes by, the leader might ask individuals whether a follow-up course on "spiritual resources" would be helpful, what ingredients they would like it to contain, what format it should take ("Would a shared meal be a good idea?"), when it should meet, how often and for how long. By the time the six weeks are over, enough people may have owned the new course for it to fly.

> One group of Christians started a mums-and-tots group with a Bible story, a Christian song and lots of fun activities. The group was popular among non-churchgoers and the Christian input minimal. One of the women then invited six others to join her at another time of the week "to discuss spiritual things".
>
> They agreed, so she said something like this. "If we are going to meet together, don't we need some material to get us started? Jesus has been revered as a great spiritual leader. Why don't we start with some of the spiritual stories he told and use them as a jumping off point? We don't have to agree with them. But at least they might spark some ideas."

Spirituality is on many people's lips. They are interested in prayer and in a "higher" dimension to life. The Christian tradition has a wealth of spiritual resources that non-churchgoers may find helpful. Making them available could be a brilliant act of service. One minister's wife has on her business card, "Spiritual consultant". It opens doors.

The *Essence* spirituality course contains material that could be adapted to the group and resource its exploration. Other courses, available from Christian bookshops, could be used as follow-ups.[15] There is enough material, if suitably adapted, for a group eventually to learn how to pray, study the Bible, worship and live out the Christian life.

Discovering what will work for the group, using resource material flexibly (if it is used at all) and allowing the group to develop at its own pace could be the basis of "just-in-time church" – a church that emerges when seekers are ready.

Reaching "GenX"

Here were some options for reaching "GenX" discussed within St Mary's Church, Upton.

The first is to start with a small group of ten Christian adults, drawn from GenX, three of whom are in leadership. During the week, the group would meet weekly in a home to pray, form good relationships and plan. Members would continue to attend one of the Sunday services.

They would soon start a monthly social to which each group member would bring a non-churchgoing friend. During the social, one of the group would welcome people and briefly describe what it means to belong to this group of Jesus' disciples.

As two or three friends show interest in the Christian faith, they would be invited to one of the weekly small-group meetings. The meeting would become a monthly enquirers' group, perhaps eventually meeting twice a month. "Everything turns on the quality of our relational life, and on the depth of our understanding of the issues that are important to our friends, as seen from a Christian perspective."

The second is to launch with 15 Christian adults, three in leadership. From the start, three small groups would be formed, with the aim that each should grow to 10-15 members within two years.

One group would support the church's work among unchurched 18- to 35-year-olds on an ex-council estate, seeking to draw some into discipleship within the group. Another would use its own friendship circle to invite one or two people at a time into the group, exposing them to some corporate Christian life. A third would offer a monthly evening of spiritual exploration, based loosely on the *Essence* course.

Each group would meet at least fortnightly for prayer, planning and mutual support. All three would combine every six weeks for a more organised time of worship and prayer, with some teaching input from the wider St Mary's leadership. Members would not necessarily attend the Sunday services.

The third is to form an action group to bridge the social divide. The group would work with the least privileged young adults in Upton – for example, through political lobbying, a small credit union to relieve debt and a relationship skills course.

Group members would get to know people very different to themselves, and mutual respect would develop. In due course, the group would sponsor a guest concert once a quarter, to which those linked to the group's activities would be invited. A clear gospel message would be given as the basis for all the group does. That would be the first step toward a group in which individuals could explore the Christian faith.

Why will it keep on?

"What will go on?" and "How will it move on?" are important questions. But "Why will it keep on?" is perhaps the most difficult. Many fresh expressions have looked promising at the start, only to flounder later on.

The initiative by St Michael's Blackheath, described in Chapter Two, seemed poised to flourish when George Lings wrote his account of it. But soon afterwards its leader, Conrad Parsons, left. A member of the St Michael's congregation was appointed on a one-day-a-week basis to continue the work. But he was distracted by difficulties at home and in his work. The venture stalled. It now limps along, a mere whimper of what seemed possible a few years back.

Burnout can be a killer in emerging churches. New expressions can take a long time to mature, they can be hard work, they can prove disappointing, relationships can fracture and the pioneers' own circumstances can become fraught. Sustainability is perhaps *the* biggest challenge for fresh expressions of church.

A planning group would be well advised to douse its ideas with realism and ask, "As the initiative kicks into gear, what can we do to ensure it is sustained – that it will keep going on?" Certain things can help.

Don't skimp on resources

One of the most important is to make sure the venture is adequately resourced. Will the leaders get adequate support? Will they receive regular input and training? Will they know where to find appropriate resources? If volunteers lead the team, what will happen if a key member has to pull out? If the leader is paid, will funds be available to renew their contract and/or to pay for a replacement? How many of these "i's" need to be dotted in advance, and how far can God be "trusted" to cross the "t's" as they are reached?

Keep it simple

Another key is to travel light – to keep church "low maintenance". The inherited church can be awesomely complicated. Sunday worship can be resource-rich, demanding time and preparation. Then there are all the other activities! Breaking away from copy-cat church may include looking for simpler models.

These may include meeting less often. Why not meet only as frequently as people have the energy? Better perhaps a sustained monthly event, which slowly draws people in and builds up resources, than a weekly meeting that rockets and fizzles out.

Gatherings do not have to be complicated. A post-*Alpha* group growing into a church, for example, might start with a meal where half the group take it in turns to bring a dish – "enough for me and one other". After chit-chat, candles on the tables might be lit, and recorded Christian music might create a context for quiet prayer and worship.

Participants might be invited to discuss a Bible passage, as they remain seated at their tables. "What do you find most interesting? What can we learn from it? Is there anything that would make you behave differently?" The questions can vary from session to session. Individuals might then share concerns, from items in the media to crises at home or work, and these could be taken up in silent or spoken prayer.

Simple objects can become symbols that inform sharing and prayer. Members of one group brought memorabilia of their early life – photographs, dolls, posters, t-shirts and books. Each person put the object at the centre of the circle, explained its significance and then the group kept silence for a while, reflecting and offering to God what had been shared. At the end they spoke of what had touched or challenged them.

Space might be left in the meeting for planning, to avoid a special committee on a separate evening. Why shouldn't planning be at the heart of worship, a matter for prayer and thanksgiving?

As the group matures, members might be expected to meet no more than once a week. If small groups come together, the larger gathering might meet fortnightly and the smaller groups during the intervening weeks. Leaders might form one of the small groups, once again to avoid an extra meeting.[16]

Value each phase

Because emerging church may take a long time to mature, focusing too heavily on the destination can make the journey seem interminable. You can end up anxious about whether you'll ever get there, worrying more about ticking off the milestones than enjoying the scenery. Valuing each stage of the group's life is imperative.

So if the starting line is a group that has no Christian input, it makes sense to be clear that what the group is doing is valuable in itself. Are people having a good time? Are they being supported? Are their lives being enriched?

If you are convinced by each phase of the journey, it will matter less whether the group reaches your hoped-for goal. You can rejoice that God is active in the group as it is, that you are making good friends and that people are valuing the experience – that spice is being added to lives which might otherwise feel bland. If the group stopped tomorrow, it would still have been worthwhile.

Plugging into the wider church

One danger is that fresh expressions of church will plough furrows entirely separate from the mainstream. That may be because the continuing church is unnecessarily suspicious. Or perhaps pioneers of the new have little time left to strengthen links with inherited church.

Yet connecting to the wider church is important not only for theological reasons, but also for practical ones: the wider church can help to sustain a new expression of church. Travellers into faith, for example, are often encouraged when they go to a Christian festival or a large gathering and discover many others who have made a similar pilgrimage – "I never knew there were so many Christians!" They return re-energised.

They will also be helped to mature in the faith by getting to know more established Christians, experiencing different styles of worship, listening to a variety of Christian speakers, and accessing Christian courses, CDs and books. Being in touch with other parts of the church is vital. Believers can paint their faith in richer colours, while responsibility for discipling new Christians can be more widely shared.

Tying into the wider church will help emerging Christians to move from one form of church to another. Individuals' circumstances may change, or believers may be drawn to a different expression of church as their faith matures. They may "shuffle" through several expressions of church during their lifetimes. Being aware of alternatives will help individuals plot a path through church, finding gatherings that suit them. They will be less likely to give up if a particular diet of church no longer feeds their spiritual growth.[17]

Keeping on track

The continuing church sometimes fears that a fresh expression will go off the theological rails – even worse, that it will become a mini tornado, out of control. There is no "100%" solution to this. The New Testament makes clear that the very first leaders of the church struggled with the same danger.

To minimise the risks, churches might ask:

- *How far do we trust the leaders involved?* Choosing the right leaders, obviously, is the best guarantee that the new venture won't run amock.
- *How are we going to support these leaders and hold them to account?* In particular, do we have a clear set of values and goals that will frame this accountability? Have we been explicit about what can be renegotiated as the initiative proceeds, and what is an irreducible minimum? Do we want the accountability to be mutual – with leaders of the new venture holding the parent to account for providing adequate support? If so, how?
- *How can we ensure that as people come into the faith they will be properly rooted in the gospel?* For example, where self-discovery methods of learning are used – "Get into a group and discuss why this passage is relevant today" – how can we avoid the blind leading the blind? This may be a particular issue if the leader of a new venture has little theological background.

  Answers may include inviting the minister or an experienced lay person to teach the emerging group from time to time. Showing a videoed sermon from another congregation might be a possibility. So might corralling suitable resources. For instance, in a gathering that used small-group discussion rather than a sermon, Bible study aids might be put on a table for the groups to plunder. Or someone might be invited to read the aids in advance and act as a consultant to the groups. Offering the leader(s) some theological training could be a good idea!

- *What arrangements will we make to ensure that the venture is connecting to the wider church?* This will include doing things with the sending congregation from time to time, but – hopefully – it will extend beyond that: to attending Christian concerts, conferences, retreats and so on. This will help new Christians access some of the wisdom of the wider church and develop a more rounded faith. A pub, a pint and a prayer does not equal church.

Within a newly minted church it will be vital to keep the original values and vision to the fore. They should be explicitly communicated to newcomers who start to attend regularly – "We thought it might be helpful for you to know what we are about and why."

Mission, in particular, needs to be constantly taught and practised. Church does not exist for the individual Christian, nor for itself, but to serve the surrounding culture and help transform it.

The three selfs

To go the distance, a toddler church needs to mature and become self-sufficient. This may involve some form of the classic three "selfs":

- *Self-financing.* New expressions will need support from the inherited church at first, but as new members learn to give generously they should become progressively self-supporting. In time they should contribute financially to the parent, to the wider church and to new offspring they are planting themselves.
- *Self-governing.* Prolonged dependence on the sending church can stunt initiative and prevent emerging churches learning through taking responsibility. St Paul was not a control freak. He handed over the day-to-day care of his fledging congregations, and trusted the Holy Spirit and the

new leaders to move the work forward.

- *Self-propagating*. Success for a church plant can be an alba-
  tross – "We've done it. Now let's concentrate on building up
  those who are here." Fresh expressions are not to become
  like existing congregations. They are not to become so
  absorbed with their own journeys to God, so spiritually
  bloated, that they have little energy to do it again. New
  plants should reproduce – grow, not swell.

Stuart Murray Williams writes:

*Should we expect all forms of emerging church to become
progressively self-supporting? What about children's
churches or churches for homeless people? Maybe some
expressions of church will only last for a few years before
completing their mission tasks? Are longevity or financial
self-sufficiency necessarily signs of ecclesial authenticity?*

Learning from the experience

"Learning organisations", "the knowledge economy", "learning networks" – everyone knows the message: learning has
moved to the heart of our society. So it should not be surprising
if learning also becomes the nub of emerging church.

The church is breaking new ground. It is vital that all expressions of church learn from each other to be inspired by what's
worked, to avoid repeating mistakes and to refine their theologies. Smart experiments are as important as new experiments.
Watching these experiments can reveal what God is doing.
"There's no such thing as failure – only feedback!"[18]

So it is important that new forms of church share their
experiences. Websites like www.emergingchurch.info and
www.opensourcetheology.net offer a way of doing this. So do
occasional conferences and informal networks. As pioneers
share their stories, they will not only support others: they will
forge networks that can bring advice and encouragement in
return. "Good news" and "lessons learnt" stories may help
inherited church to become more comfortable with the new.

Valuing the small

Individual churches can incorporate emerging church into their everyday lives. No blueprint exists, but churches wanting to be involved might ask: "Who's the initiative from?" "Who's it by?" "Who's it with?" "What will go on?" "How will it move on?" and "Why will it keep on?"

Not all fresh expressions will spring from an individual church. Yet if emerging church is to haul the inherited church out of its castle, where it is doing a Sleeping Beauty while the world passes by, fresh expressions will need to become part-and-parcel of congregational life. This may seem a far cry, but enough examples exist to know that it is entirely realistic – and is starting to happen. Emerging church need not be divorced from the continuing church: it can become a better way of being an existing church.

Many examples of "new church" are small. Are they too small to offer much hope of "re-Christianising" Britain? The parable of the mustard seed reminds us that big results have tiny beginnings. Throughout church history, revivals have always started small. The church itself began with just one person.

Many of today's churches have tiny congregations, and often it is these churches that are growing most rapidly.[19] So we should not be discouraged by the smallness of emerging church. Indeed, it may be a cause for thanks: discipling two or three new Christians is a lot easier than 20 or 30!

Perhaps the test of a new expression of church is not the numbers involved, nor the speed at which it develops, but quite simply, whether Jesus is present at each stage of the journey.

Notes

1. George Lings and Stuart Murray, *Church Planting: Past, Present and Future*, Grove Evangelism Series 61, Cambridge: Grove Books, 2003, p. 21.
2. Groups wanting a blow-by-blow account of the steps they

could take to prepare and start a new expression of church may get ideas from Bob and Mary Hopkins, "Practical Steps and Insights for those Planning a Plant", www.encountersontheedge.org.uk. It should be noted that this is a fairly old paper, with traditional church plants mainly in mind, but it is useful nevertheless.

3. George Lings, "The Eden Puzzle", *Encounters on the Edge*, No. 14, The Sheffield Centre, 2002.

4. George Lings, "Unit 8: Out of sight, out of nothing", *Encounters on the Edge*, No. 2, The Sheffield Centre, 1999, p. 17.

5. The Shaftesbury Society has developed learning circles to encourage good local practice in church and community development.

6. For more information see, Mark Griffiths, *Don't Tell Cute Stories: Change Lives*, London: Monarch, 2003.

7. *Youthwork,* September 2002, quoted by John Hall, "The Rise of the Youth Congregation and its Missiological Significance", PhD thesis, University of Birmingham, 2003, p. 421.

8. Martin Robinson and Dwight Smith, *Invading Secular Space: Strategies for Tomorrow's Church,* London: Monarch, 2003, p. 105.

9. George Lings, "Stepping Stones", *Encounters on the Edge*, No. 18, The Sheffield Centre, 2003.

10. *The Door*, the Church of England's Oxford Diocese, March 2004.

11. Martin Raymond, *The Tomorrow People. Future consumers and how to read them*, London: FT Prentice Hall, 2003, pp. 13–16.

12. www.emergingchurch.info.

13. Tearfund, Shaftesbury Society and many denominations have practical, how-to-do-it schemes for conducting a church audit. These are structured ways of listening to a community and hearing God through it.

14. Jeanne Hinton, *Small and in Place: Practical Steps in*

Forming Small Christian Communities, Kew: New Way Publications, 1998, pp. 29–31.

15. Some of these are becoming very accessible and imaginative – for example Scripture Union's *Connect Bible Studies* includes "What does the Bible say about..." studies on Harry Potter, Madonna, James Bond.

16. This is based roughly on some of the experiments at St Thomas Crookes, Sheffield.

17. This certainly raises questions: is it too consumerist an approach to church, or is it a realistic recognition that people change a lot in our fluid culture and may need different expressions of church at different stages of their lives? Is it consumerist church, or church that is contextualised to twenty-first century culture?

18. Graham Horsley, "Church Planting – Dealing with Weakness and Failure", www.encountersontheedge.org.uk. Graham's sound bite is broadly true, but there have been exceptions – the Nine O'Clock Service, for example.

19. Bob Jackson, *Hope for the Church*, London: Church House Publishing, 2002, p. 109.

CHAPTER EIGHT

FAST-TRACKING NEW CHURCH

Emerging church deserves more resources because it is an agent of mission, a fundamental calling of church; its values can be rooted in the character of God; changes in advanced society are bringing it on to the agenda; it makes good strategic sense; it has the potential to subvert consumerism; it frees the imagination by rattling caged-in assumptions about the nature of church; and ordinary churches can do it.

It is beginning to appear on the must-do lists of denominations and "streams" (which are networks of churches). This chapter argues that fresh expressions of church should be at the top of those lists – not just another tool in the kit for improving the church, but a "must-have". Leaders should make emerging church a priority and lead from the top, mobilise support for it, shift resources into it, build the capacity to undertake it and develop new networks to underpin it. The future of the church depends on decisions taken now.

Making it a priority

The strategic importance of emerging church is percolating through to denomination and stream leaders. The idea is winning support – slowly. But getting the resources will be much harder.

Top of the in-tray

Attitudes range widely. Some leaders of denominations and streams question the seriousness of the drop in church rolls. They believe they should keep sailing the same course because people will return to the faith when the bankruptcy of modern consumerism has been exposed. In the 1990s some denominations like the Baptist Union saw church attendance rise, with clear evidence of growth through new conversions.[1] "There may be life in the old dog yet."

Others leaders accept the gravity of the situation, but wonder if emerging church will be a noisy sprint up a blind alley. Emerging church seems risky, with only limited evidence of missionary success. Ploughing resources into it might suck the oxygen out of the existing church. Some have doubts about the theology involved.

Still other leaders can see a role for emerging church, but question their ability to make innovative church happen. They don't see many levers to pull. They are drained by heavy workloads and drained by institutional roadblocks. They think the most they can do is to give permission to innovators on the ground. "Perhaps I can fan a groundswell of change."

Others again would like to do more, but are not sure how. What strategies would work? Would they be supported? For many people emerging church is new, unfamiliar and a little scary. Some ministers run down their rabbit holes – "it's not what I was ordained for." Promoting emerging church would require resources – "Who would pay?"

Despite these objections, a small minority of leaders are eager to push ahead. What holds them back is the need to take others with them.

The clock is ticking

So why should denominations and streams make emerging church a priority? First, mission is at the heart of God. The church is most like God when it engages in mission. Mission is a prime reason for the church's existence.

Second, continuing as we are could spell "operation certain death". There is no guarantee that the church will survive in large parts of the advanced world. One look at the size and age of many congregations should be warning enough. There is not the slightest evidence that people are turning away from consumerism to traditional church in significant numbers. People may be interested in spirituality, but that does not equal church.

The slice of Britain's population with any church background – perhaps three-fifths in the 1990s and just one-fifth in some urban areas – is shrinking fast. Generations that were brought up in the church are passing away. Fewer children are in the pews – in the UK 35% in 1940; a mere 4% in 2000. That leaves 96% outside church![2]

The church has to prepare for a completely different mission context. Christians can no longer call "old friends" to return. In a few years the great majority of people will have no ties to church at all – no memories for church to appeal to.

All the anecdotal evidence points in the same direction: thriving churches, with seemingly effective evangelism, flourish mainly because they attract individuals with some church experience. Few churches are making headway among those with no church background. Yet this will be soon – if it is not now – the "mission field" in Britain. If the church does not develop ways of reaching the non-churched today, it will enter this daunting world strategically naked.

Although some denominations and streams have grown recently, the figures may be skewed – for example, by a disproportionate number of younger congregations (which often find it easier to grow). In the case of the Baptist Union, some large and rapidly growing African churches in London have boosted the count.

As these growing congregations "grey" and older members pass away, how will these "healthy" denominations and streams avoid chasing the others into decline? After growing in the

1990s, Baptist church attendance is expected to be heading firmly downward by 2005.[3]

There is nothing inevitable about the continuation of church. Once-thriving churches – in North Africa for example – have withered away. What is at stake today is the very future of the Western church. Why cling to the past when it no longer works? "A clear and present danger" should be a priority for any leader.

How many businesses would willingly entrust their future to a product in decline? They would diversify into more promising opportunities, and spread their risks. When many people are quitting church and fewer are coming in, why put most of our eggs in the existing church basket?

The principles of emerging church address the new situation and are theologically well founded. They also have the potential to bring together community development and evangelism. Often resources within the existing church are not used to their best effect because these two strands of mission have been kept apart. Church social action will vanish into history if Christians who support it evaporate too.

Yet time is against us. As congregations age and shrink, the resources for new initiatives will shrivel too. The church should have changed direction years ago. Even so, better far the new forms of church come to the boil past their teatime than not at all. Experiments are urgent.

It has been said that the Church of England never misses an opportunity to miss an opportunity. Is the Western church about to sleepwalk into near oblivion, or will this generation lay foundations for Christianity's recovery in the next?

We need more church planting – of the right kind

Third, emerging church is more than a lightening bolt flashing across the zeitgeist. To those who doubt that it is the answer to emptying pews, Chapter Four presented evidence that church planting can work. A number of teenage and youth congregations, such as Eternity in Bracknell near London, have well-established track records. Other fresh expressions, such as Cable Street Community Church in east London, have shown durability and growth.

> The 1990s saw the greatest growth in the number of Elim churches and those attending them since the 1930s – from 437 churches in 1990 to 592 in 1999. Church planting played a significant role in this, although the denomination also grew through existing churches joining.[4]

We also know that many church plants have not worked, largely because they have been of the wrong kind – they replicated obsolescent models of church.[5] This has made them too complicated, putting a strain on leaders, and perpetuated the stand-off between church and today's culture. We need church planting of the right kind.

Even if individual experiments "fail", we still need to learn how to apply emerging church principles. Disappointments, as well as successes, will be good teachers. Better for denominations and streams to be actively engaged – and to foster learning – than to be bypassed by innovations that leave the inherited church behind.

Denominations can make a difference

Fourth, denominations and streams need not be crushed by their heritage: leaders can bring about change. The renewed emphasis on planting by the Elim churches, for example, was ignited by putting church planting into the brief of regional superintendents, as well as by the role of Kensington Temple in London.[6]

Twenty years ago, the Church of England hardly had any youth ministers. It took the initiative to establish four centres where youth workers can now be trained to degree level for ministry within the Anglican Church and other denominations. Youth pastors can't be churned out fast enough – a number are experimenting with new expressions of church. Vision within a denomination made a difference.

After an initial phase of church planting, the Assemblies of God reviewed what they had done. One of their conclusions was that

> a programme of transformative church planting demanded the transformation of the denomination as a whole. Changing one significant area in a system carried the implication of changing everything. To their credit, the Assemblies of God have not abandoned church planting. Instead, they are facing the challenge of transforming the denomination, not least of all in terms of the training systems that are used. They are committed to the refocusing of their existing congregations towards mission, and have engaged around 100 congregations in a programme of mission discovery entitled "Journey into Mission". They recognise that this requires a commitment for the long haul.[7]

Stuart Murray Williams writes:

Denominations can also make a difference by funding emerging churches. An example, as Mike mentions later in the chapter, is the Anglican Diocese of Oxford, which has launched its "Cutting Edge" initiative with a mixture of central funds and additional money raised specifically for this project.

But can denominations champion emerging church when they are cutting back staff? As congregations have wound down, collection plates have looked empty and paid ministry has been chopped back. Church reorganisation is difficult enough to take on board, some think, without picking up emerging church as well.

In practice however, it may be easier to retrench if fresh forms of church are part of the package. Many churchgoers despair because cutbacks seem destined to be followed by more cuts. Strategies to reverse decline seem scarcely to scratch the surface. "If we go on as we are, but with fewer resources, why should what has failed in the past work in the future?" After the reorganisation is complete, post-match exhaustion sets in and little is done to prevent another round of cuts.

Emerging church offers an approach that is new enough to give hope, but not so difficult as to be out of reach. One of its attractions is that it can be small-scale and simple. Might fresh expressions be the vision element that helps reorganisation click into place?

Led from the top, released at the bottom

"My job is simply to bless innovations on the ground." This view is surprisingly widespread among denomination and stream leaders. They think the most they can do to encourage emerging church is to give permission.

Giving permission – is that it?

Yet permission-giving alone will not be enough. To be effective, it will need to be supported by evidence that fresh expressions of church can work. In any organisation, perhaps a quarter of the people welcome change, the same number are hard-wired to resist and the rest could go either way. Those who are "up for" emerging church need arguments and data with which to convince their colleagues.

This strengthens the case for some kind of "ginger agency", discussed later. The agency would research the evidence-base for emerging church, spotlight what works and splash around the results. Leaders would give permission for change: the agency would help innovators to gather support.

But even with this support, might "letting the flow flow" be too limp-wristed a strategy, especially given the fragile state of low-ebb church? How many head teachers, for example, have turned round a school merely by "blessing" good practice in the classroom? Effective heads take the lead in introducing best practice, coaching and mentoring teachers, and providing a clear vision for the staff to work toward. They don't vaguely point to a path: they strike out ahead. Much the same is true of other organisations. "You don't get to be a leader by being a tracker."

Leading change

Getting a balance between "top-down" and "bottom-up"

change is a titanic challenge. Some experts advocate a "life cycle" approach. Different leadership styles will suit different stages of an organisation's life.

At a certain point, strong leadership from the top may be needed to secure a fundamental change in the organisation's culture. Individuals don't always want to leave their comfort zones. Top-down leadership may be required even for something as straightforward as encouraging staff to network: leaders may have to press down to push staff out.

When the change has bedded in, a different and more hands-off style may be appropriate. Staff may need scope to innovate bottom-up. Perhaps later the need arises for another dose of top-down leadership. The world has changed – yet again, and the organisation needs to take a further quantum leap.

Organisations require leadership that is sensitive to the different stages of their lives. Someone who is brilliant at introducing change from above may need to move on when a different style is necessary. Organisations need wisdom to recognise what style is appropriate when they make key appointments.

Might some denominations and streams be at the stage of their life cycle when strong, top-down leadership is vital to bring about active support for fresh expressions of church (a real challenge for denominations that are highly decentralised)? A more laid back and delegated approach may be appropriate later on.

Navigating through this complex world, with little in the way of maps, is a formidable task. Many of the tools of "top-down, bottom-up" leadership have yet to be developed. How "from below" and "from above" fit together is not always clear. Much will be demanded of those in the top spots.

Like their secular counterparts, church leaders will find that getting change to ripple down, up and across will remain one of *the* challenges ahead. Key leadership words will be collaboration, empowerment, persuasion and opportunism along with decisive, clear, strategic and values-based. Charting a course through opposites of this kind is the "symbol and brand" of the postmodern world.

A new priority?

Giving time to emerging church will not be easy for leaders with more than enough on their plates. Might denominations or streams consider creating an extra post for a limited period? The new appointment could lift some work off the most senior staff, leaving them with more time to lead the denomination into fresh expressions of church.

Adding posts to the central organisation is not wildly popular! Yet no one else will have as much capacity to mobilise change as the person at the top. Freeing that person up could yield huge dividends.

Should leaders reconsider their priorities? Some, for example, have acted as "chaplains" to the wider community. This brought many benefits when the church had a dominant place in society and its leaders a prominent role.

In "post-Christendom" the church is being pushed to the margins – indeed, in some areas its very future is at risk. A different theology of engagement may be appropriate.[8] Perhaps denomination and stream leaders should spend less time connecting with society at a regional or national level, and more time equipping churches to engage with their local communities and networks.

The church is close to the brink. So renewing its grassroots involvement may be more strategic in the long run than shoring up its crumbling presence higher in society. Maybe a platform can be built now for the church to have a stronger regional and national presence in the future. If leaders short-change the foundations of the church today, how far will the church be able to engage with society – at any level – tomorrow?

Stuart Murray Williams writes:

Emerging churches may be needed at all levels of society, but grass roots churches on the margins and among the marginalised may be the most significant. This is counter-intuitive in relation to past mission strategies, which so

> *often targeted the top and hoped for a trickle-down impact,*
> *but it chimes in remarkably well with the biblical story of a*
> *God who breaks in from the margins.*

Mobilising support

Denominational and stream leaders can do much to unleash emerging church by putting the case for it – in meetings with individuals, in committees and other forums, and when they address larger gatherings.

Advocacy will spread awareness and help to put fresh expressions of church on the map. It will give permission to those who might be inclined to experiment. It will help pioneers get support – "If the bishop or superintendent wants it, so should we." It will encourage churchgoers to back emerging church with resources. It will mobilise the denomination or stream.

A problem for many church leaders is that part of their calling is to represent the people they lead, both opponents and supporters of change. Each group needs to be able to identify with their leaders. Senior staff may become cautious lest they get too far ahead of the pack.

Spending time with people

Yet many leaders do combine their representative role with pro-active leadership. Often they echo Jesus, who was extraordinarily radical but built a large following. How was he able to move ahead of the people, and yet stay close to them?

One reason was that he immersed himself in the people's lives and served them. He ate and mixed with all sorts. He spent time with them, even when he wanted to be alone. He healed their sick. He reached out to those on the edge of society. Ordinary people knew he was on their side – and so they trusted him. When leaders are trusted, they can afford to challenge their followers.

As some do now, being pro-active about emerging church may require senior staff to spend time with fellow clergy and lay leaders, encouraging them to explore the principles of emerging church, helping them to work through what it might mean in practice, mobilising the resources of "the centre" to support them (which will mean meticulous attention to key appointments) and helping to bump away the barriers – "Are your lay leaders feeling hesitant? Why don't I host a day conference for them and help us to address the issues?"

Creating dissatisfaction

One person asked, "How do we persuade people who quite like things as they are?" Part of the answer, perhaps, is to help them feel the Arctic blast of church decline – to remind people of falling rolls, to keep explaining why the church cannot go on as it has, and to combine this chilling message with the vision for an alternative.

Some church leaders have sought to keep up morale by declaring that things are not as bad as they seem. But this can be counter-productive. Alongside the complacent are churchgoers who know that things *are* as bad as they seem. Perhaps they have heard that their full-time minister will not be replaced, or they ask, "Who will be left when we've passed on?" False optimism makes some in the pews wonder if their leaders are in touch. Others conclude that their leaders don't know what to do, which makes them even more depressed. As for the complacent, they won't change until they feel the alligator nipping at their heels.

At the heart of Jesus's message was repentance – dissatisfaction with the status quo. He could encourage this dissatisfaction because he had a better alternative. As some are doing, leaders can send a similar message about the existing church: they can promote discontent, but avoid despair by offering emerging church as a new direction.

> *George Lings writes:*
> *I hope this book will be a significant way in which the fog of denial is blown away and the grey skies of despair find that a sun is shining through the clouds. Discomfort is not*

a bad place to begin. Often it is how the Holy Spirit announces his presence when individuals are being prompted to change. Why can't that be true for churches too?

Telling the story

Jesus put his message into the context of Israel's ongoing history. After the resurrection for example, on the road to Emmaus, "he began with Moses and all the prophets, and explained to them the passages which referred to himself in every part of the scriptures" (Luke 24:27, NEB). This is a story he had affirmed throughout his life. He had attended synagogue regularly, observed the Jewish festivals, been to the Temple and publicly signed up to the law. People knew that their story was his story.

A vision for emerging church will be more persuasive if leaders can tell a vivid story, easy for time-pressed members to understand, about why new forms of church are necessary, how they can come about, how they fit into the denomination's or stream's history and why they are important for the future.

The story may need to answer: "Why was the stream or denomination founded?" "What was its original genius?" "How can fresh expressions of church build on the divine deposit we've inherited?" "What values within continuing church will be reproduced in the emerging forms?"

Almost certainly, the story will need to affirm the existing church. A "both-and" approach – both current expressions of church and new ones – avoids expecting everyone to change, values what already exists and ensures church members are not asked to give up what is precious to them.

Creating space

Jesus gave space for people to reach their own conclusions. Though he could be direct with his critics, he taught in parables, which allowed individuals to explore what he meant and the implications.

In today's individualistic culture, leaders may be wise not to be too prescriptive. Perhaps they can invite churchgoers to enter into the problems of the continuing church, explore the options and examine different ways of being church. Winning support for emerging church would be consistent with the methodology of emerging church – "bottom-up".

The transformation of Gillette® is instructive. By 2001 it was clear that one strong product was masking the underlying weakness of Gillette®. The company needed to be turned around. Chief Executive Jim Kilts began the process by opening dialogue, putting abundant facts on the table, setting norms that blame could no longer be shifted to anyone else and giving people frequent performance information. Employees could make up their own minds on the basis of the facts.

Providing an experience

Finally, Jesus immersed his followers in the life he was offering. He formed his disciples into a community based on his teaching, and taught them to practise what he was doing – to heal the sick, announce his coming and baptise converts into his repentance.

Emerging church is so foreign to the experience of many clergy and lay people that teaching the theory may not be enough. Indeed, teaching alone can disempower people – "I need to do something different, but I don't know how." A "sheep dip" experience of what might be involved can be highly effective.

> Chris Neal in the Church of England's Oxford Diocese invited ten key clergy and others, who were "up for it", to join him for a week away. He gave them an experience of what community could be like, to envision and enthuse them. Participants were challenged to explore how the experience of church could be made many times better.

Shifting resources

Advocacy is vital to persuade continuing church to put resources into fresh expressions of church. Best intentions will come to nothing if they are not matched by money, volunteers and new priorities. This painful shift will only occur by convincing churchgoers of the need. How might resources be redirected?

Catalysts on behalf of a denomination or stream

Just as there is no one model of emerging church, no single way exists to channel resources into it (see following section). Emerging church could be encouraged by catalysts working on behalf of a denomination or stream, or by catalysts on behalf of a group of churches within the denomination or stream (perhaps working ecumenically), or by catalysts within individual churches.

Some denominations have appointed a minister to establish a "network church", which appeals to a particular group of people rather than a specific area. *The Net* in Huddersfield, for example, aims to work with postmodern seekers, mainly friends of the 30 or so planting core, who want to participate rather than observe and still remain anonymous. *B1* in Birmingham seeks to reach the 20s and 30s age group. Both are Anglican.[9]

Large initiatives can showcase a different way of being church. They can touch groups that the existing church hasn't reached – young people for example. They can be geared to those most estranged from the church. Leaving fresh expressions purely to individual congregations may allow the latter to cherry-pick easy areas and networks, neglecting the most difficult.

A not-to-miss opportunity will be the new housing estates springing up over the next 20 years. The UK Government plans that just over 2.2 million new homes will be built in England between 2003 and 2016.[10] This would boost the number of dwellings by roughly a tenth in a mere 13 years!

Bigger estates will offer a chance to try something new. Experimental church on a major development could take the sting out of the fear that resources are being drawn from the existing church. The denomination would have wanted a new church there anyway.

Different ways to resource church planting

Runners are like a strawberry plant, which sends out a shoot nearby. A new expression of church may have close ties to its sending church, which provides most of the resources. But close links to the mother church have tended to produce plants that are similar to the mother: diversity has been less common. Runners are great if you want to produce another strawberry plant, but not much use if the aim is runner beans!

Grafts are like a shoot introduced through a slit cut into another stock. A plant is introduced into a church building, often alongside another congregation. This may be intended to revive the mission of the original congregation, or to supplement it.

Transplants are like taking a large garden plant, dividing it and replanting part in a new location, so that the parts have more space in which to grow. Perhaps 50 or more people from one church or more move to a new location and start afresh. Initial support may come from one or several churches, or through a denomination. The plant's size enables it to become self-sufficient quite quickly. Yet hopes for the plant are often dashed. Sometimes the planting group becomes more preoccupied with its own needs than with reaching out.

Seeds are like plants that spring up from a tiny seed blown some distance from its host. The initiating team, usually small, may move home to start a new church, crossing traditional church boundaries. The plant may take considerable time to grow. Because team members are some distance away, their home churches may have little ownership of what they are doing (though this is not always the case). Financial support may come from friends, a mission agency or a denomination.

Based on *Mission-shaped Church*, London: Church House Publishing, 2004, pp. 113–15.

> The Anglican Diocese of Leicester has appointed a minister to work on a rapidly expanding housing estate. It will be his first job after his initial training post. He has been given a house and a laptop, and a brief to pioneer fresh expressions of church on the estate. He will have a support group of senior clergy, who will hold him to account. Part of the advice he has been given is not to be tied down by preconceptions of church, and not to be over-encumbered by church structures.

But "showcases" also have drawbacks. If the experiment runs out of steam, as with *Tommy's*, an Anglican network church in Nottingham, the failure will be all too visible; it may set back the cause of emerging church. If the venture starts with a sizable and heterogeneous core of 30 plus, perhaps drawn from a number of different churches, it may be hard to focus on a specific network. The friends of the core may be too disparate to draw them into a stable community.

Most important, showcase experiments risk letting everyone else off the hook. Individual churches may think "emerging church is not for us, it's that experiment over there"; opportunities on their doorsteps may be missed. The experiment may be seen as drawing resources from the existing church, rather than the mainstream starting to use resources more effectively.

Might "showcases" be combined with a seedbed approach – little initiatives scattered throughout a denomination or stream?

Catalysts on behalf of a group of churches

How might experimental seeds be sown? One possibility would be for a group of local churches within a stream or denomination, or jumping across denominational boundaries, to appoint someone to scatter the seeds on their behalf. It could be a new appointment, or an existing post with a new role.

These catalysts could help individuals to explore new recipes for church among their friends and contacts, within groups on the church fringe, or in the wider community.

Or catalysts might lead a fresh expression themselves, especially within neglected networks spanning several churches. This would not be quite the same as a denomination or stream venture: the initiative would have come from a group of local churches rather than higher up in the denomination, it might not start with a specific plant in mind and a smaller core of Christians might be involved at the start.

> In early 2002, for example, Mark Berry began work within the Church of England as Mursley Deanery's youth worker. His role includes experimenting with new ways of being church among young people. The aim, in his words, is to plant the gospel rather than just church, and see what grows. A group of 16–20-year-olds meet each Monday "to eat, chill, discuss and worship together" in an informal setting, with different people taking a lead. The group seeks to be a steering and visionary group for mission and worship, to develop young leadership training and experience, and to give a sense of community.
>
> Mark spends much of his time in a secondary school, building relationships. "The school is aware that our vision is to grow church as a community of seekers, within the school community and are fully supportive of this." Spirituality is a hot topic in education and provides a way in. "We have initiated a weekly space/drop-in to share stories of spirituality; this is an inclusive space, hosted by Christians but not a club for Christians. We have experienced an incredible depth of spiritual quest . . . Non-Christian young people think of church as an institution, not a spiritual community. We hope to share our God stories and to nurture their spiritual searching.'[11]

If funding is not available, a group of churches might start with a suitable volunteer. Such people do exist – for example, early-retired teachers, people working part-time and unpaid clergy who see mission as their main job. I can think of at least one recently retired bishop who would be up for it! As the work expands, the churches may be able to produce a quarter salary and then a half.

It might be wise not to be too prescriptive about what the person – paid or unpaid – should do. Better perhaps to let them create their own groove than to imprint one for them. After all, emerging church is bottom-up, and churches' expectations of a pioneer should reflect that.

The challenge for streams and denominations is to create space within their structures for entrepreneurs. Catalysts need to be held to account and properly supported. But if they are tied down with too many meetings and commitments, they may be squeezed out of the existing church altogether. It is easy for the church's immune system to reject seemingly foreign pioneers.

Catalysts within individual churches

Rather than launching an initiative itself or encouraging a group of churches to appoint someone to act on their behalf, a denomination or stream might promote the idea of catalysts *within* individual churches. Possibly this could be built into reorganisation schemes involving the redeployment of clergy. Certainly it could be part of the denomination's or stream's overall strategy. Among the possibilities:

- Trainee clergy could be asked to spend half their time on a fresh expression of church. As suggested in Chapter Four, for example, if a Church of England diocese received five full-time curates in a year, initially one might be appointed to a church that had a fresh expression in mind. If this worked, the number could be stepped up to two, and then more perhaps. If all the curates did it, the diocese would be launching five new expressions of church every twelve months![12]
- A church with a paid youth worker, children's worker, minister or other staff might be encouraged to include in their job expectations, "Spend two days (maybe) on emerging church and three days on the existing church." This might not be the calling of existing post-holders, but the new expectation could be built into a job as it became vacant.
- A church might be encouraged to re-designate an existing post, as in St Mary's Upton, so that emerging church is

more than a part-time focus: it becomes the full-time job of a staff member.

Full- and part-time staff would be freed up to work with volunteers and innovate on the church fringe and beyond. Cutbacks in some denominations mean that a new breed of "mini-bishops" is emerging – full-time clergy who oversee a number of churches, a few with paid staff. These ministers might oversee experiments with church, as part of their wider role. But will they be secure enough to release others?

For years people have talked about the importance of mission. Yet until this is a clear expectation of ministers and other paid staff, written into job descriptions where they exist, the shift from maintenance to mission will remain an empty phrase.[13]

Releasing resources

Change is speeding up in several denominations. The northwest region of the Salvation Army, for example, plans an imaginative programme of church planting. The northern synod of the United Reformed Church persuaded 300 of their members to discuss new ways of being church. The Church of England is debating whether to reallocate a chunk of its historic resources to fresh expressions of church, though the idea has met with considerable opposition.[14]

In November 2000 the Church of England's Oxford Diocesan Synod committed itself to "creating new forms of emerging church". The Diocese is offering:

- A framework of support and accountability, to encourage those planting new Christian communities and to root these communities firmly in the life of the Diocese.
- A process of mentoring and review to ensure that "lessons learnt" can be shared.
- Financial stability by devoting new resources from the Church Commissioners to "Cutting Edge Ministries", to be augmented by

money raised within the Diocese.[15] Financial support for new
Christian communities will be wound down gradually over five and
occasionally seven years, as the communities become self-
supporting.

To qualify, new initiative must show:

- An understanding of mission and church – "We are not looking for
  projects but rather for new expressions of church."
- Developmental possibilities – for example, "How will you build in
  sustainability?"
- Leadership – for instance, "What is your approach to risk-taking?"
- Accountability – such as a willingness to share in mutual support
  and learning with others in the Cutting Edge Ministries. "Are you
  willing to work in an accountable, creative relationship with your
  bishop?"

"Our vision is that by 2010 we will have up to eight of these new
'emerging' churches in the Diocese – self-sustaining in their life,
finance and ministry – acting as an inspiration to others."

Financial support for emerging church may come from additional giving (not easy), from redirecting reserve – or "historic" – funds (in only a few cases) or from refocusing existing posts. Some resources may also become available from mission agencies that see the strategic importance of a multi-pronged church in the advanced world. A key question will be how to sustain the continuing church on a slimmer budget.

Super-sized churches, which pioneer new expressions themselves, could eventually play a key role – in minster mode.[16] They could share what they have learnt with smaller churches, provide a coaching and mentoring service perhaps, and possibly offer some seed funding as well.

A question hangs over many big churches: do they pull their weight in reaching the growing number of people who have no church connections at all? The contribution of large churches is potentially huge. So denominational leaders may want to spend time with them, seeking mutual understanding of each other's visions, problems and needs. Might a strategic convergence between the two evolve?

Releasing resources will be painful. But can a bulimic church be cured in any other way? With the Western church getting thinner and thinner, isn't new life better than a slow death?

As resources switch to emerging church, denominations and streams may be wise not to hail every success as "the new way forward". That might cripple future experiments. We are entering a period of watching, waiting and learning.

Building capacity

It is common for organisations to ask: How do you amp up the capacity of staff to innovate, change and achieve more with existing resources? The challenge for streams and denominations is to increase their capacity to develop new forms of church.

A hierarchy of expectations

Just as the job expectations of staff on the ground need to change gradually, so do the expectations of those in the structures of denominations and streams. Imagine that everyone in "the hierarchy" had "encouraging emerging church" in their job description. Priorities would shift dramatically!

For example, children's, youth and community workers might be given the tasks (among others)

- of working with individual churches to encourage fresh expressions of church among children, young people and others in the community;
- of coaching, mentoring and overseeing a team of church planters, drawn from individual churches;
- of developing "learning networks" among those planting new forms of church;
- of occasionally being part of a team that was launching a new venture.

One responsibility of a superintendent or archdeacon might be to facilitate emerging church – helping to unlock bureaucratic gridlock and sometimes providing oversight. Even a finance officer might be expected to encourage new forms of church. Instead of just warning against the difficulties of redirecting funds, their job would become "How do we overcome the financial obstacles?"

Such a radical change of emphasis is a universe away from where we are now, but might it suggest a direction in which to travel? Each vacancy could be an opportunity to refocus the post in support of emerging church. Some of today's preoccupations of course would have to drop off the list or be done in other ways, which would be painful. Yet won't going on as we are be even more painful in the long run?

Coaching, counselling and mentoring

Ministers and others trying new forms of church will often require support and advice. Texas-based Emerging Church Network has identified this as a clear need.

> It is building up a team of assessors to help local churches answer the questions, "Who are the various culture groups? Where, in the city, are they? Who is within reach of existing churches and who is outside the scope of their reach? Who are the emerging leaders who can be trained to implement the strategy?" The Network aims to provide "the education, on-site training, community and mentoring that emerging leaders need to be healthy and to have the 'tools' to build churches that will transform lives and communities with the love of Christ.'[17]

One possibility might be to invite, say, ten churches at a time to sign up for a series of training sessions over a year, involving their minister and fellow leaders. Over the following two or three years, ongoing mentoring could be offered to churches that completed the course. The Church of England's Liverpool Diocese runs a School of Leadership on these lines.

Building on their Sheffield-based church planting school,

Bob and Mary Hopkins have piloted a coaching course to train others to coach and support leaders of emerging church. Coaching can be a more effective means of learning than attending a course. You learn what you need, when you need it, in more manageable chunks than by attending a whole course, much of which you forget. In the jargon, it is "just-for-you" learning "just-in-time", rather than "just-in-case".

The demand for coaches to support fresh expressions of church is ballooning.

> One doctor attended Bob and Mary's church planting school. He returned to Lincolnshire and started an inter-denominational course for 20 people in the first year and 40 in the second, drawn from twelve projects. Leaders from each project meet with leaders from two or three different projects every six weeks for an evening. Three coaching teams, including the Hopkins, resource the meetings.

Selecting and training entrepreneurs

Mission-shaped Church called on the Church of England to identify and train leaders for pioneering missionary projects. Its recommendations could apply to the church at large. Specifically,

- such work needs to be recognised as a specific call. The qualities required may differ from traditional ministry. They need to be clearly identified, so that appropriate candidates can be selected for ordination or recognised as having a lay vocation;
- specialist training needs to be available in each region;
- lay people with appropriate gifts need to be identified, trained, recognised and authorised;
- training needs to be provided in context.[18]

Do we need new kinds of people to be involved with training – trainers with the capacity to equip individuals for emerging, not just the inherited, church? Do these people exist? If not, how can we add to their number?

A ginger agency

Some experts are asking whether reform of Britain's public services might be achieved through trusted, independent bodies that research best practice and communicate the results. Information would spread about what works well, encouraging "modernisation". Might this suggest a model for the church?

We've noted that in any organisation some people want change, others are implacably opposed and most are somewhere in between. Supporters of change need ammunition. They need hard evidence that what they propose will produce better results than the status quo. As this evidence piles up, people who are undecided will gradually support the case for change and be more willing to make the sacrifices involved.

An agency that encouraged research into the "growth hormones" of emerging church and fanned out the results would strengthen the hands of those who welcome the new. It would boost the effectiveness of learning networks, and support trainers and coaches. The research might include case studies, such as those produced by the Church Army's Sheffield Centre, quantitative research into best practice, such as the work Bob Jackson has begun to do, and theological reflections on developments in emerging church, such as those by Bishop Graham Cray and Stuart Murray Williams.

The Church of England is moving towards a national initiative on these lines. If funds are available, the initiative might have a small number of full-time staff, supported by a larger team of advisers. It would serve the church by helping to discover new ways of being church. Might other denominations and streams do something similar, either on their own or jointly?

The priority at this stage is probably research and advocacy rather than training. The church has all sorts of people with training skills. What these trainers need is research into what has worked and what hasn't, what lessons can be learnt, what successful practices can be replicated and what can't, what theological questions are raised and how they might be answered. A few eye-popping successes would not go amiss.

Sustaining the new

Start-ups can soon run out of fuel. To get momentum, account-ability is obviously important. So too is support through coach-ing and networks, financial backing for a while perhaps, and continuity of leadership, especially at the beginning. Turning emerging church into a continuing church calls for the long haul.

In a Church of England context, George Lings suggests some helpful signs that a new initiative is authorised.[19] They include (slightly adapted):

- The mission risks were applauded in official letters and wider communication.
- Such documents affirmed that cross-cultural mission could lead to culturally attuned worship and governance.
- The leaders were affirmed, authorised and financially assisted.
- A succession of leadership beyond the pioneers was promised, should the work continue to flourish.
- An appropriate legal existence was found, with mission driving the lawyers, not the other way round!
- Accountable relationships exist with others in the denomin-ation or stream.
- The emerging church is appropriately represented within the stream or denomination.

The aim should be to help the venture become self-financing, self-governing and self-propagating – the holy grail of church planting.

As the group settles down, leadership requirements can change. Initially a willingness to take risks, try something new, build networks and commend the faith may be all-important. Later a stronger priority may be to pastor the members and support their discipleship. The original entrepreneur's gifts may be used best in a new initiative, with someone else leading the group to its next phase.

This conventional wisdom, however, runs the risk of encouraging the group to become too settled. The group may move from mission mode to maintenance, and fail to reproduce. The inherited church has not been conspicuously successful at combining mission with maintenance. Will emerging church fare better?

Getting the benefits of scale

Organisations are changing rapidly. As we have noted, many are personalising their offerings. Often this involves working in partnership with clients or customers to determine how the product can best fit the individual or segment of the market.

New forms of church are doing something similar. Christians work with the group or network to develop an expression of church that suits the context. At times we have talked about "bottom up" church. But the church can never be totally bottom-up. A dialogue takes place between Christians and emerging believers to contextualise the new expression of faith.

The shift to a more personalised world stares us in the face. But what is often ignored is that you can't deliver personalised products without reconfiguring scale.

Creating critical mass

Traditional economies of scale enabled "vertical" organisations to integrate "under one roof" legal, personnel, marketing and many other services. If you produced enough products you could cover the costs involved. These old economies of scale are no longer enough: new forms are needed alongside them.

Typically, they are "horizontal" in nature. For instance, organisations work together to create the critical mass that enables them to reach a specific group. An example would be the idea being mooted of schools cooperating in an area, so that each develops a specialty that caters for children with particular gifts. Collaboration ensures each school has enough gifted children to make specialising possible.

Something similar is necessary for emerging church. Individual churches may not have the resources to reach a particular network. They may have to work with each other, perhaps across denominations. This has been the basis of a number of youth churches: instead of several churches each having a tiny, perhaps rather "sad" group of young people, the groups are brought together to form the nucleus of a larger and more vibrant gathering.

Resource material

Critical mass will be especially important for the production of new resource material. As new waves of church emerge, the demand will grow for material to support groups exploring the Christian faith. The need will range from material suitable for people with no Christian background to material that can help with Christian discipleship. Much material already exists to support evangelism within the continuing church, but it is not always suited to fresh expressions of church.

Emerging church is becoming ever more diverse. So the more material available, the easier it will be for groups to find what fits their particular context. Catering for this diversity will be a financial challenge. The market may become so fragmented that producers find it difficult to secure enough sales to cover their costs.

It could make sense for denominations and streams to network together, in conversation with Christian publishers. They would collaborate to identify needs and how to meet them. This might avoid each stream or denomination producing their own, heavily branded material, duplicating what was already available and fragmenting the market still further. Economies of scale could be combined with more targeted material.

The scope for putting resources on the Net is immense, as is happening with alt.worship. How about an "emerging church" portal, which individuals could enter like a high street and find all the resources in one place?

Fuller church

"Horizontal scale" also occurs when firms combine products to offer a more bespoke package – such as a pharmaceutical company selling its products within a supermarket. An enhanced service is delivered to an identified group of customers. Sometimes companies compete on the one hand and collaborate on the other!

Churches may need to think "cooperation" if they are to create a fuller expression of church for emerging (as well as existing) Christians. Might one church in an area organise adult education courses to help people grow in the faith, another arrange a Saturday club for children, another in-depth prayer for healing, and a fourth marriage preparation classes? "Boutique" churches would combine their offerings to serve the whole Christian community in the locality.

This may seem a journey-to-Mars away from the sturdy silos that exist now. But can the church go on as it is? The scale dimension is often neglected in discussions about emerging church, but it is vital. Many fresh expressions of church, as with older ones, will be too small to allow individuals to mature into a rounded faith.

Churches may need to cooperate to enhance opportunities for fellowship, to offer prayer retreats and discipleship courses, and to provide worship at different times and places to fit individuals' fluid lives. Merging alongside emerging church is a theological necessity, certainly – but also a practical one.

Learning networks

A further example of horizontal scale is the use of learning networks – either formal or informal. Networks are springing up in the secular world as a major source of knowledge and mutual support. For example, American-based TEC facilitates regular meetings of senior executives in over 40 small groups around the UK. Participants share the pressure, and learn from each other as they discuss problems brought to the group by each member.

Denominations could encourage similar meetings of emerging church leaders. They might meet face-to-face perhaps every couple of months, with contact online between meetings. Members could share experiences, seek advice and develop friendships. From time to time, these learning circles might consult someone with particular expertise – in conflict management for example.

> A group of larger churches in the Midlands have met with a team of missioners in a series of day conferences over the last three years, exchanging church-growth ideas between themselves. By 2003 they seemed to have reversed their long-term decline, recording a combined attendance growth of 6%. Key to their growth was that half of the churches involved opened up a new worship opportunity or congregation during 2003.

The need for learning is urgent. It goes beyond courses within theological and Bible colleges. The prime need is not for "you come to us" training in our college, but – in line with the emerging church ethos – "we'll come to you. We'll provide training and support where you are, in a way that matches your circumstances and at times that suit you."

Knowledge will flow most rapidly when training takes place within a network. What's learnt will ripple out through word of mouth. Independent trainers, or missioners and others employed by a denomination or stream, may have more flexibility to provide this kind of support than training colleges.

Stuart Murray Williams writes:

Another example of a learning network is Urban Expressions Associates – a network of urban church planters involved in emerging churches in various cities in the UK and other nations, linked through a website (www.urbanexpression.org.uk) and committed to sharing

> *stories and resources electronically and through face-to-face gatherings.*

Issues of identity

New forms of scale are shaping what is required from leaders in the wider world. Vertical organisations, often slimmed down, now exist alongside horizontal networks. Individuals may be employed by the former, but also belong to the latter.

This means that secular organisations have a continuing need for leadership that gives direction to the vertical organisation, clarifying its values and holding people to the vision. At the same time, space has to be created for individual initiative. As networks proliferate and information becomes ever more abundant, command and control becomes increasingly difficult. Individuals have to be given discretion to gather information, sift it, form appropriate teams and act upon it. This calls for a high degree of trust and clear parameters within which employees can act.

Many secular organisations are decentralising fiercely to give individual units the freedom to adapt to a world that can change in a heartbeat, and to network with other organisations as appropriate. Frequently this raises questions about what holds an organisation together.

The church will face similar questions. Not least, how culturally specific can a new expression of church be without betraying values fundamental to the denomination or stream – or worse, to the Christian faith? As horizontal networks across traditions become steadily more important – from Christian festivals to ecumenical coaching for emerging leaders – what will be the continuing role of well-established streams and denominations?

All fall down?

Broadcaster and commentator, Malcolm Muggeridge, once likened ecumenism to watching the pubs turn out at night. Everyone held arms, because if they didn't they would collapse into a heap.

Fresh expressions will struggle to stand up – they may even fall down – if churches fail to cooperate with each other. Christians have excellent reasons for working together. Are they going to be left behind by the secular world? If not, who will lead the new forms of collaboration that are becoming so vital?

What if? Three futures for church

Denomination and stream leaders should make fresh expressions of church a priority. They should lead from the top to release fresh expressions at the bottom. They should mobilise support for emerging church, for shifting resources into it, for building the capacity to deliver it and for collaborating across traditional boundaries.

How the church is led over the next few years will determine the sort of church this generation bequeaths to the next. What might church look like in 20 years' time? We conclude with three scenarios (possible futures).

Key influences

The scenarios will be influenced by a number of factors, but key drivers for change will include:

- The continuing decline of the existing church, despite efforts to shore it up.
- The existence of mission opportunities in our fast-changing consumer culture.
- The continued fragmentation of society – different expressions of church will be required to reach different niches.
- The tightening squeeze on people's time, which will create an appetite for "simple church".

But there will also be barriers to change.

- The inherited church may be paralysed by its own weaknesses. Some over-stretched ministers will be too exhausted and traditional to embrace change. Ageing lay members may lack the energy to initiate change themselves. In some denominations, maintaining buildings will be a continuing drain on resources.

- The new collaborative networks needed for emerging church may fail to materialise. Distrust, the time involved and disputes over second order issues could get in the way. Churches may fail to cooperate to create the critical mass required to support some fresh expressions of church. Many churches will remain reluctant to pool resources. Learning networks may be a low priority.

- Fresh expressions of church may be "taken over" by existing churchgoers with weak mission hearts. Emerging church may become a way of keeping current members in the fold rather than serving the wider society.

- In many cases, leadership within denominations and streams will be inadequate.

How might these drivers and barriers blend together?

More of the same

This is the first scenario: the church continues to slide into oblivion in much of the country. As their feeder churches shrivel up, large churches begin to struggle too. The weaknesses of the inherited church, reluctance to cooperate and poor leadership combine to dampen new initiatives. Fresh expressions of church are not sufficiently numerous to reverse overall decline.

There are a few bright spots, mainly among recent immigrant communities. Many new arrivals have Christian backgrounds, and help to keep the church alive.

Plausible though it is, however, almost certainly this is the least likely scenario. The forces for change will be too great. As churches stare into the abyss, the jitter index will shoot off the page and they will refuse to go on as they are. Where there is strong resistance to change, entrepreneurs will abandon denominations and streams, and go it alone.

Isolated experiments

In this second scenario, denominations and streams wake up to the need for new expressions of church. Slowly and painfully leaders support experimentation not just with words, but with some resources too. Emerging church gets a higher priority in the selection and training of ministers. It becomes received wisdom.

Change is driven by the parlous state of the existing church, by emerging mission opportunities, by the new cultural mood that privileges diversity and by time-squeezed churchgoers, who demand a more simple church. A new generation of denominational and stream leaders make emerging church a priority, and in some cases have the skills to lead rapid change.

But fresh expressions fail to realise their mission potential. First, many are captured by existing churchgoers. They end up as a new way of being church for those who already come. The mission imperative is weak.

Second, where fresh expressions do connect with people outside church, they become a series of monads, isolated fragments in space. Churches of all kind fail to cooperate, pool resources and attach a high priority to learning networks. Denominations and streams squabble over matters of secondary importance. A poor theology of "Church" discourages individuals from sinking their differences and putting effort into collaboration.

Informal networks continue to emerge, but not often enough or on the scale required to enable new forms of church to really blossom. Many experiments with church are isolated and poorly supported by the wider church. Pioneers keep repeating others' mistakes because they are not learning from their peers.

For most of the time, new believers have a narrow experience of church, which stunts their spiritual growth. Eventually, a significant number feel dissatisfied and leave.

Hyphenated church

In this third scenario, as in the previous one, emerging church rises up the agenda. Resources are put into new experiments. Many fresh expressions meet the demands and aspirations of the surrounding culture.

What distinguishes *Hyphenated church* from *Isolated experiments* is that the church successfully uses scale to support emerging forms, and these forms connect with the surrounding world. Individual churches cooperate to create new expressions of church in schools, among networks in the social mainstream, and among poor and homeless people.

They pool resources so that increasingly churches in a locality specialise – one majoring on midweek training, another on the environment and a third running a bereavement call-in centre, for example. Each specialisation serves the whole church in that area. New arrivals in church have a much richer spiritual experience than in the previous scenario.

Learning networks become a priority. Those leading fresh expressions meet frequently together and keep in touch online. They help each other problem-solve, spread best practice and often become mutual support groups. Lessons from one experiment are quickly transmitted to another. The momentum for emerging church continues to build.

This scenario would require radically new attitudes. Is it impossible? Or might the urgency of the mission situation – the demise of the existing church and the opening up of new opportunities – bring it about?

A made-over church?

Emerging church need not be daunting, it need not be out of reach. It is a different way of thinking about church. Its values reflect the character of God. It is on the agenda because society at large is changing. It makes good strategic sense. It has the potential to breed Christian communities that help consumer society be more community-minded and inclusive. It asks questions that could free the church from straitjackets on mission. Most local churches could do it. Denominations and streams could actively promote it.

The church will not reverse decline by continuing with the methods that brought decline. It needs a fresh approach – one that allows more people to have authentic encounters with Christ. As we hurtle down the century, emerging church offers practical ways of being new kinds of church for a new world, changed communities that can change society.

Notes

1. Baptist church attendance rose from 267,000 in 1990 to 280,000 in 2000. Peter Brierley (ed.), *UK Christian Handbook. Religious Trends 4*, London: Christian Research, 2003, p. 2.24. But see also footnote 3.

2. *Mission-shaped Church*, London: Church House Publishing, 2004, pp. 36–41.

3. Projections for 2005 suggest numbers will drop to 276,000 from 280,000 in 2000. Brierley, p. 2.24.

4. George Lings and Stuart Murray, *Church Planting: Past, Present and Future*, Grove Evangelism Series 61, Cambridge: Grove Books, 2003, p. 9.

5. Ibid., p. 16.

6. Ibid., p. 9.

7. Martin Robinson and Dwight Smith, *Invading Secular Space*, London: Monarch, 2003, p. 82.

8. There are some complex issues here, which are explored, for example, by Stuart Murray, *Post-Christendom*, Carlisle: Paternoster, 2004.

9. For an account of both, see George Lings, "Net Gains", *Encounters on the Edge,* No. 19, The Sheffield Centre, 2003.

10. Kate Barker, *Review of Housing Supply. Interim Report – Analysis*, London: HM Treasury, 2003, Chapter Two. Whether the Government's target will be met is a moot point.

11. www.emergingchurch.info.

12. Another possibility would be for the trainee minister to be half time with an existing church and half time starting

emerging church on behalf of a group of local churches, though this risks two half-time jobs becoming two full-time ones! Another possibility would be half-time tent-making and half-time church planting.

13. Obviously this assumes that people with the right training and aptitude are recruited in the first place!

14. *Future Use of the Church Commissioners' Funds. Report by the Spending Review Working Group of the Archbishops' Council and the Church Commissioners*, London: General Synod of the Church of England, 2004, pp. 21–33. Whatever the conclusions the Church of England reaches, like other denominations it will have to think creatively about how it deploys its funds.

15. The Church Commissioners' funds were from a previous allocation, not the new allocation that has been proposed.

16. The potential of minster churches is discussed, in a Church of England context, by Nick Spencer, *Parochial Vision. The Future of the English Parish*, Exeter: Paternoster, 2004.

17. www.emergingchurchnetwork.com.

18. *Mission-shaped Church*, op. cit., pp. 134–35.

19. George Lings, "Joining the club – or changing the rules?", *Encounters on the Edge*, No. 5, The Sheffield Centre, p. 25.

AFTERWORD:
WHAT'S IN IT FOR THE POOR?

My colleague, Mike Moynagh, pleads for the church to emerge in new ways into an uncertain future. I am grateful for his ongoing urgency to express what is apparent in the UK, namely that the church is in tatters but that God is at work forging new forms of Christian community.

With Mike there is a profound combination of the pragmatic realist and the visionary evangelist. He sees the present darkness but senses the approaching light. Our response to the book should be to get out and get on with the task of mission and evangelism.

For myself and other urban practitioners who find their context for church in city environs, the key question is, *"What's in it for the poor?"* The book refers to the notion that the church will emerge amongst the urban poor. But how will this happen?

If, as Mike hopes, Christians will take note of and take hope from the book, they might re-enter the context of mission with fresh insight and vision. If, as I dread, Christians will read the book, selecting theologies for their own context and deselecting the poor, as so often happens they will re-enter the context of mission to widen the growing gap between the "have nots" and the "haves".

So let's attempt to apply the thinking about emerging church to the poor.

1. What might theology look like from the viewpoint of the poor?

The gospel has always emerged from the poor. The question about how the poor will fare is one that quickly gets to the heart of the value system behind any new idea or method. It is a question that flows through both Old and New Testaments, applying God's good news to the poor as well as to the universal nations.

Both Jewish and Christian faiths resulted from peoples under pressure seeking to make sense of their world. The cult of Yahweh re-emerged in exile to become a dominant mission to the Israelites and then to the nations. The sect of Christians emerged when their leader was killed, resurrected and reappeared to send his followers out into the world. In both instances, the resultant faith formed a community out of the embers of pain.

These new religions prioritised the poor, not merely concerning themselves with issues of their own identity or survival. It is this reflection that describes my desire to apply the book in the context of the poor.

In a nutshell, it is totally apparent to the poor that God has identified himself with them in the person of Jesus. The Christ-event is about solidarity, a meeting on the level in a place of earthly pain. From here, Christ leads his people to resist the oppressor, to stand against the tide of disillusionment and oppression.

The poor understand Jesus to have laid aside his glory and his power in order that he might be fully human. It is a theology of incarnation.

2. What might emerging church look like from the viewpoint of the poor?

At first glance, the poor are not likely to be interested in church in that, so far, the church has tended to favour the well off and the established. Traditionally, the church has prospered in areas of affluence and this is still the case.

At a second glance, the poor will note that what has disempowered them has been top-down church, the rigid and hierarchical religion of a bygone age. Emerging church can be "level church", one in which the class differences are over-ridden, where the cult of the expert makes way for the cult of the discoverer. Mike writes about "bottom-up" church that eschews the hierarchical.

Where a church takes the incarnation of Christ seriously, with its leaders living in the area where the church is situated in houses like everyone else, then an applied gospel is seen in action. This church does ministry amongst the poor and not to the poor. It listens to the experience of the poor and responds accordingly. Urban Expressions, quoted in the book, is a good example.

A hallmark of such a church in the urban heartlands of Britain is for it to be *a church that includes*. In a multiracial area it will have a mission policy to make different cultures welcome.

> At St Stephen's Church in Hyson Green, part of Urban Nottingham, a project called the Rainbow Project exists to attract the church towards a rainbow vision, one that reaches out to people of different colours, ethnicity and experience. It works with Christians of African, Caribbean and Asian backgrounds, with Christians in black majority or Asian churches and with other faiths that live in the area. It is hardly surprising that this vision is leading the church into a wider ministry that engages with asylum seekers and people on the margins. It is hardly surprising that this policy is leading the church into growth, as the word gets around and more people gather, united by the common experience of being different yet of believing in inclusion. It's an example of Mike's plea for church to arise out of community initiatives.

Another hallmark of such a church is that it *will reach out to the young people* that are always to be found in the city.

In St Peter's Church in Radford, an urban priority area church in Nottingham, the unattached children outnumbered the adults by a long way when the congregation found that the local children loved the mysterious old building, its shelter from the cold and its tins of biscuits. Over a period of time, as this church accepted the unlikely ministry of an elderly congregation towards children, the numbers of children grew and grew. Church members used their resources to attract funding and other help from link churches. Before long, a youth group had formed, as well as regular provision for children in the main services. This was an emerging "youth congregation", because the youth were beginning to gather their identity and become identifiable as a worshipping focus within the "mother church".

In some urban areas, it has become *impossible to maintain existing church buildings* and the local congregation have opted to use the local school as a worship base, eventually building strong links and finding themselves to be a mission partner with the school. This was happening long before the Dearing Report was published in 2001, in that many churches have found this a new means of not only surviving but developing new mission objectives, potentially becoming "school-linked church".

Probably the most common feature of emerging church on the margins of society is that described in Anne Morisy's *Beyond the Good Samaritan* (1997). Here she describes churches in poor areas that *re-invent themselves by noticing their surroundings* and beginning to serve their communities. At times they emerge with "network-focus church" and sometimes with "revamped traditional church" but always with an "apt liturgy" that suits the congregation as it reaches out into the community.

Probably the most talked about form of emerging church in the area of poverty is "Base Community Church", a form of church *arising to empower* poor people by a process of liberation in which the poor are mobilised and form their own strategies. Examples of such churches exist in Glasgow and in other major cities, though they are often sub-cultures to wider church bodies.

3. Can emerging church benefit the poor?

In a recent mission seminar with students from St John's Nottingham, I asked them to consider twelve forms of emerging church. After reflection, they were to consider how each model benefited the rich and how each benefited the poor. (They worked under the assumption that the rich were those who could "buy a pizza if so desired" and the poor were those who were socially excluded.)

In each instance the students were able to easily identify benefits for the rich . . . more choice, more stimulation, more creativity, more challenge etc. To identify how the poor would benefit was a harder question. The prevailing cry was, "*It all depends how you set up your new form of emerging church.*"

In other words, emerging church, in and of itself is neither beneficial nor excluding to rich or poor but it is likely to be naturally applied to what we understand, to be interpreted in ways that make it most easily accessible to the rich.

It was noted that cell church, for example, generally flourishes in areas where boundaries are understood and adhered to. In places where social skills of engagement are lacking, where people have not learnt how to listen to the other, to exchange ideas and to be committed to the other, and where relationships are transitory and people are constantly moving home, it is more difficult to set up a group that is accountable to itself. By very definition, the excluded do not do groups, they do not know how to form emerging church.

Using the example of emerging church in an inner city where like-minded people gather to serve a project such as a homelessness centre, it is conceivable that the carers will meet to pray and to support each other. But it is less likely that the church will attract the homeless unless in a dependency inducing manner. Why is this? It is simply because the inequalities of cultures between the homeless and the home-dwellers would be virtually insurmountable.

The idea of a church that attracts people from every tribe and tongue and nation is extremely attractive, but where people have endeavoured to build communities for asylum seekers in Britain's cities, they have met with the problem that asylum seekers have vast needs that cannot be fully or even partially met by an emerging church.

To serve the needs of a group of vulnerable and needy people, in a way that is not going to develop an unhealthy and permanent dependency, necessitates a highly resourced core group of disciples who interpret their mission as reaching a key target group. Such a project might well end up succeeding, but only if the core group identify their own needs as well as the needs of those whom they serve.

Of course, the opposite can happen when the core group changes. In one city, a project that reached out to asylum seekers ended up being run by asylum seekers who had attained resident status and then went on to boost the sponsoring church. Indeed, in many churches that have reached out to welcome asylum seekers, they have found that their congregation has grown and their mission objectives have been enriched.

> My favourite example of this is that of Mother Teresa who reputedly would open the gates of the convent in Calcutta at 5am and would serve the poor and the hungry until 3pm. On some occasions, those who had starved to death would have to be moved from the gates when they were opened in the morning. Mother Teresa would say that she and her nuns could not serve the needs of everyone all the time. The reason why she maintained a window of service (and did not have the convent open all the time) was in order to allow her nuns to pray and to play. She saw this as following in the steps of the human Jesus who sometimes saw the crowds and responded by going up the mountain to pray. In other words, Mother Teresa was able to set up a form of emerging church that benefited the poor because she also cared for the needs of her team and herself.

4. Is it possible for the church to emerge amongst all types of people?

Before God, I hope that this is so because the gospel is a universal gospel and Christ is God's chosen instrument to access humanity. The question is how?

This issue most powerfully impacts on my consciousness as I reflect on Pete. Pete had been part of the inner-city church at which I attended. He had played with children from that church from childhood. He had been involved in uniformed organisations, he had helped in the services, he had known the acceptance of that church in many ways but he had never felt that he truly belonged. Last week (from the time of writing) Pete took his own life.

Every night since then I have ruminated on how things might have been different. How might Pete have been made to feel included? The only answer that has impacted me has been that coming from another Christian teenager who knew Pete. He said, "Don't get this wrong, but Pete never stood a chance. The guy was a geek. Sure we liked him a bit but he didn't look right and he had no brains. He was not the guy you'd include as a real friend." So that was it, Pete was not included at a very deep level.

My personal question remains, can there be a church for the likes of Pete? Will Christians ever get to a point of having enough energy to invest in someone who is less attractive and who offers fewer returns? If the answer is "yes", then I wonder how many such people can be loved by a small group. How many people with special needs would it take to swamp a cell? What is the capacity of a small group to survive if it makes its target those who are vulnerable? Can emerging church grow up to serve the church (that body of Christ for all) as well as to serve itself?

Maybe the answers to this will be found if Mike's work is taken thoughtfully and reflected upon theologically. In other words, if this book is read prayerfully and considered in the wider context of a globalising, urbanising world, it will be released to generate mission that is holistic, containing aspects of justice as well as of worship.

My desire is that I act as a "government health warning" that notes the value of a product only in so far as it is used correctly. In other words, this book is crucially important, but must be part of a wider discussion that endeavours to resist the individualising tide of postmodernity. In conjunction to such work there needs to be a sense of the relational tide of the mission of the whole church.

Emerging church is a gift of God as he works through his church. It is a continuation of the work of the Holy Spirit operating as the mission of God in the world. It is our task to ensure that this mission is expressed through justice and action as much as through worship and prayer, and as much through the whole people of God as through the individual expression of one unique individual.

The tree will be known by its fruit and that fruit will be evidenced by its commitment to the poor, as well as to others.

Revd Dr Howard Worsley
Director of Studies at St John's College
Tutor for Mission, Urban Theology and Contextual Theology

APPENDIX: HELPFUL RESOURCES

Some useful websites

Alternative worship (www.alternativeworship.org)
Links to worldwide alternative worship sites and provides access to resources.

Anglican Church Planting Initiatives (www.acpi.org.uk)
Advice, coaching and consultancy on church planting – not only for Anglicans.

Cell Church UK (www.cellchurch.co.uk)
Encouraging and promoting relevant cell churches across denominations.

Coaching for church planters (www.coachnet.org)
An American site for those who want online support for multiplying churches.

Emergent (www.emergent-uk.org)
Resources, information and events for those interested in, or involved with emerging church.

Emerging Church (www.emergingchurch.info)
Stories, reflection and discussion on the emerging church.

Encounters on the Edge (www.encountersontheedge.org.uk)
The site supporting the *Encounters on the Edge* series of booklets, and serving the Church Army's Sheffield Centre in Sheffield.

Open source theology (www.opensourcetheology.net)
A collaborative project to develop a transparent, community-driven theology for the emerging church.

ReSource – church plant training (www.resourcechurch planting.com)
A consortium of agencies and denominations offering training in church planting, in particular church for the variety of UK cultures.

RUN – Reaching the Unchurched Network (www.run.org.uk)
Encouraging emerging forms of church to communicate Christ to contemporary culture.

Urban Expression (www.urbanexpression.org.uk)
A mission agency that puts church-planting teams into under-churched areas of east London.

Some useful reading

Peter Brierley (ed.), *UK Christian Handbook. Religious Trends*, London: Christian Research, published annually. Useful digest of church statistics and commentary.

Graham Cray, *Youth Congregations and the Emerging Church*, Cambridge: Grove Books, 2002. Contains some helpful theological reflections.

Encounters on the Edge, Sheffield: Church Army – The Sheffield Centre. A regular series of case studies on fresh expressions of church, with helpful reflections.

Michael Frost and Alan Hirsch, *The Shaping of Things to Come*, Peabody: Hendrickson, 2003. A stimulating theological reflection on emerging church.

Robin Gill, *Churchgoing and Christian Ethics*, Cambridge: Cambridge University Press, 1999. Chapter Seven presents a useful overview of explanations for church decline in Britain.

Bob Jackson, *Hope for the Church*, London: Church House Publishing, 2002. Some interesting lessons from a statistical analysis, drawing mainly on Church of England sources. Needs to be read carefully, lest it is dismissed as a mere plea to lead existing churches more effectively.

Alan Jamieson, *A Churchless Faith. Faith journey beyond the churches*, London: SPCK, 2002. A superb New Zealand-based study of why people leave church.

George Lings and Stuart Murray, *Church Planting: Past, Present and Future*, Cambridge: Grove Books, 2003. Two of Britain's foremost observers of church planting teamed up to consult with others on the UK's experience of church planting in the 1990s.

Mission-shaped Church, London: Church House Publishing, 2004. An influential Church of England report advocating fresh expressions of church, with some useful theological reflections.

Michael Moynagh, *Changing World, Changing Church*, London: Monarch, 2001. Describes the cultural context in which new forms of church are emerging.

Stuart Murray, *Church Planting. Laying Foundations*, Carlisle: Paternoster, 1998. Still a classic, and a must-have on every church planter's shelves.

Stuart Murray, *Post-Christendom*, Carlisle: Paternoster, 2004. An historical survey leading to reflection on what it means for today's church to be in a post-Christendom world.

Pete Ward, *Liquid Church*, Carlisle: Paternoster, 2002. A thought-provoking reflection on what church might look like in the emerging network society.